CENTRAL STANDARD

To Joel,
from your old buddy.
We're far away but
still breathing. Hope
you enjoy the book.
Patrick Irelan

CENTRAL STANDARD

A TIME, A PLACE, A FAMILY

PATRICK IRELAN

UNIVERSITY OF IOWA PRESS Ψ IOWA CITY

University of Iowa Press, Iowa City 52242
Design by Richard Hendel
http://www.uiowa.edu/uiowapress

The publication of this book was generously supported by the
University of Iowa Foundation.

Title page: Patrick Irelan, age two, at the CB&Q depot in Salem, Iowa, 1945.

Printed on acid-free paper

Library of Congress Cataloging-in-Publication Data
Irelan, Patrick, 1943–
Central standard: a time, a place, a family / by Patrick Irelan.
p.   cm. — (A Bur Oak book)
Includes index.
ISBN 0-87745-830-8
1. Irelan family.   2. Irelan, Patrick, 1943—Family.   3. Middle West—
Biography.   I. Title.   II. Series.
CT274.I74I74 2002
977′.033′0922—dc21
[B]   2002021134

02   03   04   05   06   C   5   4   3   2   1

For Jane, Emily, and Claire

No story is bad if it is truthful.

Cervantes

CONTENTS

═══════

ACKNOWLEDGMENTS

I must thank numerous people, including those who read the manuscript and offered suggestions for improvement: Edmund de Chasca, Sharon Hanson, Jacinta Hart, Daniel Lechay, Coleen Maddy, James Moxley, and David Ricketts. The following people provided both information and assitance: Paulette Biedenbender, an editorial assistant at *Trains* magazine; Holly Carver, director of the University of Iowa Press, who accepted the book for publication and offered both encouragement and suggestions for improvement; Jessie Dolch, the copyeditor who corrected many flaws and spotted many inconsistencies; Jon P. Finney, auditor of Van Buren County, Iowa; Dian Gottlob, who provided legal information pro bono; LaDonna Hanes, board secretary for the Davis County Community School District and fellow graduate of the class of 1961; Elizabeth Hill, specialist in matters related to children and the family; Larry Meisgeier, living repository of volumes of railroad information; Jean Cutler Prior, a senior research geologist for the Iowa Department of Natural Resources; Judy Rowles, cattle farmer; David Widmer, who thought of the title thirty years before I thought of the book; and the staff at the office of the clerk of court for Davis County, Iowa.

Finally, I would like to thank Brian Roman, an Amtrak employee who went out of his way to find and mail to me a *California Zephyr* timetable for the winter of 1995–1996. Support Amtrak. Always travel by rail.

I never knew Grandma Susan Hudgens Irelan. I never sat on her lap and ran my fingers through her hair and over her face the way that babies do as they set out to discover the world. I never smelled her skin, thereby learning that only she emitted that exact scent, a scent that a baby can use to distinguish one person from another. Grandma Susie never read to me or rocked me to sleep. When I fell down while learning to walk, she never picked me up and cured my wounds.

Grandma Susie died on an operating table at St. Joseph's Hospital in Ottumwa, Iowa, as an anesthesiologist and a roomful of nurses struggled to keep her alive while a surgeon removed a tumor from her intestines. She was sixty-six years old on that January day in 1935, eight years before I was born, and it could be argued that she had worked herself to death and that she lacked the strength to survive a critical operation that would have saved a stronger woman.

In 1889, at the age of twenty-one, my grandmother had married Grandpa Marion Irelan, and over the next twenty-two years she gave birth to twelve children, all but one of whom lived into adulthood. During all those years, when not giving birth or caring for her own children, and for many years thereafter, she taught at the Drakesville Elementary School. Her obituary stated that "any work that needed to be done in church, home or community, she was willing and ready to help."

I have seen only one clear photograph of my grandmother. When my parents were still alive, this photograph always hung in their bedroom, watching over them as they slept. Now it hangs in my bedroom, where it protects me from all harm. And someday, if my children show good judgment and a willingness to share, it will protect them.

After my grandmother's death, the mortician took the body twenty miles back to Drakesville. On the day of Grandma's funeral, the principal closed the elementary school for the entire day so that the children could attend the prayer service, the funeral, and the burial. Grandma and her family had lived on a farm just west of town, and she had taught school for so many years that every child and adult in the town and the surrounding neighborhood knew her.

———

With those few words, I have just told you every important thing I know about Susan Maria Hudgens Irelan, the grandmother I never saw or touched. But my story doesn't end there. It only begins. For if Grandma Susie had not lived that life as she did, there would be no storyteller pecking clumsily at his keyboard. There would have been no father, no mother, no sister, no twenty-six aunts and uncles, no cousins too numerous to count. There would have been no story of my family's adventures on the railroads, in the packinghouse, on farms, in droughts and blizzards, in dust storms and famine, on the prairie and the Great Plains, and in lonely small-town depots.

The book that you hold in your hands was supposed to be about my parents, but I quickly learned that I could not tell this story without many unplanned digressions into the lives of aunts, uncles, grand-parents, and many others, long dead, that I learned about only because my parents and other relatives told and retold the same tales about these people throughout my entire life, until my father, mother, and other elders began to fall silent forever.

I have heard that the oral tradition in America is dying, largely because so many people would rather stare at their television sets than talk to their friends and relatives. I hope this isn't true. For if it is, who will tell the old stories a century from now? What man, woman, or child will remember them? And who will sing the old songs, the ballads of love, betrayal, work, despair, ruined farms, desolate towns, railroads, and brave engineers?

THE CHECK

We always met in some small brightly lit café on the south side of Ottumwa, not far from the Des Moines River, Morrell's packinghouse, the John Deere plant, Barker's Implement Company, and other factories with names I never learned. The dinnerware was heavy and indestructible. Paper napkins bulged from metal dispensers. No one bothered with tablecloths.

Aunt Thelma always joined us, along with Uncle Kenny and Aunt Lily, my mother, my sister, and assorted cousins. My father usually couldn't attend, being off in some little Iowa depot — selling tickets, decoding the mysteries of the telegraph, and writing train orders for the Rock Island Lines.

These gatherings normally took place on the weekends, though occasionally we met during the week. For some reason, I retain the illusion that these events always happened in the fall, although I know that that could not have been the case. The ostensible purpose was to eat dinner together, but by the time I was six years old, I knew the real purpose. Every session allowed the adults to do something they truly loved — fight over the bill.

I never understood why this gave them so much pleasure, but they ended every meal with the same routine. After the beef and potatoes and green beans, Uncle Kenny — tall, masculine, self-confident — would begin with a firm "Give me that" to the approaching waitress, who normally complied.

Aunt Thelma, usually soft-spoken and reserved, suddenly became aggressive. Quick with her hands, she tried, sometimes successfully, to snatch the check from him. If she failed, she invariably said, "By goshens, Kenny, I'm going to pay that." My aunt Thelma was the only person I ever heard use the expression "by goshens."

My mother made feeble attempts to compete, with lines such as "Let me pay that" or "Kenny, I'll take that." But she was no match for her older sister and younger brother. Aunt Thelma's blue eyes were flashing by then. Because she had never married and had no husband and children of her own, she had concluded that the huge salary she earned as a grade-school teacher obligated her to feed the entire Hunter family. Uncle Kenny, although the youngest sibling, was also the only boy. In some families, this fact would have automatically made him the recognized leader, but in this family his sisters had never mastered the habit of following.

If Aunt Dottla, my mother's oldest sister, had attended these ritual events, the contest would have grown even more intense; for my aunt Dottla was a formidable woman, a woman with a commanding presence. But she and her family had moved to northern California in 1947, depriving her of the rewards of these periodic battles.

So the struggle continued. With the check still in Uncle Kenny's possession, Aunt Thelma grew increasingly vocal and Uncle Kenny became increasingly resolute, sometimes gazing out the window at the elms and maples, pretending not to hear. My mother continued her futile protests, clearing her throat indignantly. Beautiful Aunt Lily, a placid Swede among these volatile Scots-Irish, sat quietly and smiled at the children, for whom this battle was the day's best entertainment.

Even after the victor had pocketed the change, the dispute continued, with the parking lot providing the setting for final arguments and promises of future reprisals. Finally, we piled into our Fords and Chevys and drove off down the brick streets through the autumn haze, content that the routine would soon be repeated, that it would never end.

———

Into this standard mix came an occasional variable, my father, Pete Irelan, home for the day from endless travel on the main line. With his black mustache, colorful tie, countless Pall Malls, and skillful telegrapher's hands, he brought new life to the contest. He was flexible and resourceful. He was courageous and daring. He did something no one else thought of.

He bribed the waitress.

His technique was as impeccable as his dark-blue suit. I'm sure I'm the only one who ever noticed, and I knew enough not to tell anyone else and spoil the fun. My mother and her innocent siblings never saw what happened, and my father would never tell.

Seventy-five cents or a dollar went a long way in the late forties and early fifties. My father, who seemed to know everyone, would say,

"Hello, Maggie," as he came through the door, taking off his gray fedora with one hand and pressing the money into her hand with the other. His movements were flawless, invisible, accompanied by the whispered phrase, "I'll take the check."

After the pie, with which he ended every meal but breakfast, he nodded casually at the waitress, who gathered herself for the final maneuver. As she bore down on the table, my father bent his arm up and back with his palm outstretched. With all the grace of a ballerina, the waitress transferred the check to my father's hand without a word and without pause. The contest ended before it began.

But not without protest. "Pete, you give me that," Aunt Thelma said with genuine irritation, snatching for the check, which my father immediately secured in his deepest pocket. "Pete, I was going to pay that," Uncle Kenny said manfully, but with resignation already on his face. My father responded to these objections by sitting there without saying a word, laughing quietly to himself, his face flushed, his eyes closed, his body rocking gently. I never saw anything bring him more joy.

Most of them are gone now — Aunt Thelma, Aunt Lily, my mother, my father, Aunt Dottla in distant California. Their century and their way of life have gone with them, and we will have to await the evidence that our way of life is better or worse. Uncle Kenny is the only one left, and not in the best of health. But before Aunt Lily died, we still went out to dinner with her and Uncle Kenny occasionally — my cousins, my sister, our spouses, our many children. We were all nice, respectable people, but we were weak imitations of our parents, and we knew it.

The old cafés on the south side were closed and dark by then, abandoned shells beside the deserted packinghouse and vacant factories, the very places where five of my twelve uncles had worked for most of their adult lives. We met instead at ugly franchises on the edge of town. The food wasn't as good, but no one complained. A meal always tastes better when someone else cooks it and cleans up the mess.

After the pie, we all agreed how much we enjoyed seeing each other again, how we should get together more often, and how we hoped that this or that relative could join us next time. Then the talk dwindled. One by one, we slid away from the table. And when Uncle Kenny picked up the check, no one said a word.

JERRY

After my mother's first child, a boy, died at birth in 1934, she would sometimes disappear for long periods from the little farmhouse where she and my father lived. Following a frantic search by my father, Grandpa Hunter, and Uncle Kenny the first time this happened, Father always knew where to look the next time.

He would drive to Hopewell, a country graveyard beside a white church on Iowa's gentle prairie, where generations of Mother's ancestors lay beneath granite and limestone markers. There he would find her, sometimes in darkness, sometimes in a pouring rain, weeping inconsolably on the grave of her unborn son.

"Come on, Jerry," he would say. "We can't bring the baby back. You can't stay here. You'll make yourself sick." After coaxing and pleading without response, he would finally pick her up, carry her to the car, and drive home, never knowing how many more times he would have to do it again.

Someone had shown the dead boy to my mother before they took him away, but she retained no memory of this. She remained heavily sedated for days and did not attend the burial. They took her to my grandparents' house, where Grandma refused to leave her side. The minister came and read from Isaiah: "The wolf shall dwell with the lamb, and a little child shall lead them." He prayed that God would comfort this woman and this family. The doctor came, but could find little to do.

My father went home only to tend the livestock, and always returned at once. He sat on a chair beside the bed and held my mother's hand. Sometimes he dozed. Grandpa told Grandma she must sleep, but she would not. Neighbors came and left food, entering and leaving by the kitchen door, without knocking, without a word.

Finally, Mother began to rally. She asked for tea, then for food. My father held her in his arms and called her "My Dearest," "My Sweet." Grandma allowed herself to rest. The minister came, thanked God for his love, and spoke of that day "when the earth and the sea will give up their dead unto everlasting life." The doctor called one last time. Grandpa filled my parents' car with gas, added oil, added water to the radiator. Grandma prepared a basket of food. Father took Mother home.

In the mysterious way that things often happen, Mother's oldest sister had given birth to her daughter Jacquelyn only thirteen days before my mother lost her son. Mother later confessed that she couldn't bear to look at her sister's child. "I didn't dislike her," she said. "She was a beautiful baby. But she reminded me of my own baby, and I couldn't bear it." It wasn't until my sister was born two years later that my mother fully recovered. From that day on, she never refused to look at Jacquelyn.

Although my mother was born in 1907, my grandparents, Laris and Austa Fleming Hunter, persisted in the nineteenth-century practice of selecting unusual names for their children. They named their first child, a girl, "Dottla." For their secondborn, they decided on the more commonplace "Thelma." For my mother, the third child, they outdid themselves. I cannot imagine what sources they consulted before arriving at "Gerata," a name I have never heard attached to any other human being. Finally, moderation returned and they settled on "Kenneth" for their only surviving son. Another son, Melvin Elwood, died in infancy.

When my mother started to grade school, it didn't take long for her siblings, cousins, and friends to see that "Gerata" was not a suitable name for a high-spirited, red-haired, blue-eyed child of the bustling twentieth century. Someone — I don't know who — decided that "Jerry" would be more appropriate, and that is the name she carried, to the dismay of her mother, for the rest of her childhood and much of her adult life.

A black-and-white photograph of her from the twenties gives the impression of a typical flapper, peeking from beneath the narrow brim of her cloche, those close-fitting little hats so popular during that decade. The photo reveals that her firm chin, delicate nose, and gentle smile were her best features. Short hair and a knee-length dress complete the image. Although the picture doesn't show it, by this time her red hair had faded to brown.

But Jerry was no Scott Fitzgerald flapper. She was an Ash Grove, Iowa, flapper: stylish but devout. Ash Grove, the village near which she lived, contained a post office, two small churches, a general store, a doctor's office, a mill, several houses, a telephone exchange where my mother sometimes worked as an operator, and a bridge across the normally calm waters of Bear Creek. A mile and a half north of town, on a dirt road, stood Ash Grove School, the one-room building where my mother and her siblings received an excellent education.

Although they could barely afford it, her parents insisted that Jerry, her sisters, and brother should attend high school in Bloomfield, the county seat of Davis County, Iowa, eighteen miles away. Every Sunday, her father took them to their rooming houses in Bloomfield, and every Friday he brought them home. In the fall and spring they traveled by buggy, in the winter by sleigh.

Each weekend, my grandmother prepared all the food Jerry and the others would need for the coming week, and together they did the laundry. Jerry's laundry couldn't have taken long. "I only owned two dresses," she said, "one for the fall and spring, and one for the winter." After her freshman year, her wardrobe improved slightly, for by then Aunt Thelma had graduated from high school and was earning the astonishing sum of forty dollars per month as a schoolteacher, and she often lent her new dresses to my mother.

Mother's high school career had a somewhat tiresome effect on my own, for as she never stopped reminding me when I entered the same high school thirty years later, "Because I had no money for movies or other amusements, I spent all my time studying." She finished second in her class, only 1.005 percent behind the valedictorian. I don't know whether the girl who finished first had money for movies or not.

While in high school, Jerry completed "normal training," a course of study designed to prepare students to teach grade school. Then, after graduation, like her two older sisters, she became a teacher in a succession of country schools — schools with names like Buttontown, Hindu, and Pleasant Hill. No other career would have occurred to her and none would have been more appropriate, for by then it had become clear to everyone that my mother was obsessed with children. She loved them. She cared for them. And as she later told my sister, she wanted no fewer than six of her own.

Although my mother's doctor knew that her children would have to be born by Caesarean section if they were to survive, he decided not to perform this procedure with her first child "because the family could not afford it." No one who heard this remarkable statement has ever been able to tell me if he feared he would not be paid or if he wanted to spare the family an economic hardship. In either case, these were the words of a man who knew nothing about my parents.

Later, with different doctors, my mother gave birth to two healthy children, first my sister, Jane, then myself. I have in my possession the original bill, dated February 1, 1936, from the Ottumwa Hospital, where my sister was born on January 18. The entire charge came to $77.50. This included fifteen days of care for my mother at $3.00 per day, fourteen days of care for the baby at $1.00 per day, $10.50 for use of the operating room, $3.00 for a laboratory test, and $5.00 for medicine and dressing. Since the baby was still inside my mother's womb the first day, the hospital generously charged one less day of care for the baby than for the mother.

As it happened, my mother owned seventy-two chickens. My father, who could not stand being in debt, quietly sold the chickens to pay the bill. For this, my mother frequently recalled, "I never forgave him." But she kept the baby anyway. I don't know what Father sold to pay the doctor. By the time I was born, both of my parents were working for the Burlington Railroad, earning enough money to avoid the sacrifice of additional chickens. During my birth, the doctor saw that another pregnancy would kill my mother, and he did what he had to. Thereafter, in the delicate phrase of that era, my mother "was no longer able to have children."

So she never got the six babies she wanted. Nonetheless, she managed to surround herself with more children than many people find conducive to their mental health. She had two of her own, thirty-five nieces and nephews, her students, the neighbor kids, and any others who happened to drop by. She knew so many children that she often confused their names with those of other children or adults. Even my name often escaped her. "Kenny," she would say to me, using the name of her brother, "hand me that bowl." Or, "Come eat your breakfast, Kenny."

As I grew older and became more like my father, I found a new way to amuse myself. "Bring me the broom, Kenny," she would say. "Here it is, Kenny," I said, handing her the broom. Whenever I did this, and I did it often, her reply was always the same: "Oh, Pat, you idiot!"

Aunt Thelma suffered from this same inability to remember my name. "Come in and sit down, Larry," she would say, using the name of one of my cousins. "Thank you, Aunt Larry," I said politely as I sat down. Aunt Thelma invariably looked at someone else in the room and said, "He's just as crazy as his father." No one ever disputed this diagnosis.

Like millions of other Americans in her generation, my mother endured the hard times that are now part of our collective memory: drought, dust storms, plagues of grasshoppers, the Great Depression, and grinding poverty that threatened to destroy both her and my father. But regardless of what happened, she never tired of children.

When her own offspring grew up and began adding to the Irelan progeny, she never refused an invitation to care for her grandchildren. She would solve their problems, heal their wounds, and laugh sincerely at their jokes. But she excelled especially well in one area: she would read to them for hours at a time, setting a standard that the children then expected of other adults. Claire, my youngest daughter, once said to me, "You're not much of a reader, are you?" She didn't mean by this that I couldn't read well, but that I didn't read to her long enough. And long enough, by Claire's standards, meant at least all morning or all afternoon, or even the entire day.

As Mother's life passed from one stage to the next, the name "Jerry" fell increasingly into disuse. To her students, she was "Miss Hunter." After marriage, she became "Mrs. Irelan." And as the use of first names replaced more formal terms of address in the late twentieth century, she became "Gerata" again, just as her mother had wanted.

But perhaps those who knew her longest knew her best. I took her to a family gathering one Sunday when she was well into her eighties. After a day of food, talk, argument, laughter, and more food, we finally stood up to go. As we walked toward the door, Chester Hunter, one of my mother's cousins, a farmer his entire adult life, walked over and put his hand gently on her arm. "Good-bye, Jerry," he said. "Glad you could be here." That was the last time they would ever see each other this side of paradise.

"Patrick," my father said when he got home from the depot one day, "whatever you do, don't ever take a job where you have to work with the damn public." I was only a boy at the time and knew nothing of jobs and the public. After coming of age, I learned the wisdom of Father's advice, but like him, I also learned that it was impossible to follow.

Having grown up on a farm near Drakesville in Davis County, Father had always wanted to become a farmer. Ask any farmer why he likes his job, and he'll say, "It's because you get to be your own boss." Ask him what he dislikes about it, and he'll say, "It's impossible to make a living."

My father graduated from Bloomfield High School in 1925, one of the worst times in the twentieth century to go into farming. Everyone knows that the Great Depression started in 1929 and continued throughout the thirties. What many people don't remember, or never learned, is that for the fifty percent of the American population that still lived on farms, the Depression began shortly after the end of World War I in 1918. One of the sad truths of economics is that war is good for agriculture, provided the bombs aren't falling on your own cornfield. Armies have to be fed before they will climb out of the trenches and stagger through the barbed wire, poison gas, and machine-gun fire. When the war ended, the value of farm products dropped sharply, leading to an agricultural depression that lasted for more than twenty years.

Being thoroughly realistic, my father completed normal training while in high school, as did my mother, intending to become a teacher in the country schools. After graduation, he then had to pass a qualifying examination. On the day of the exam, he announced to his parents that he intended to walk into Bloomfield, a distance of about eight miles, where the superintendent of schools would administer the exam. My grandfather said, "Don't do that. I'll give you a ride." But when it came time to go, as my father later told me with some bitterness, my grandfather had disappeared, apparently having forgotten about the promised ride to Bloomfield. By then it was too late to walk, and the exam would not be given again for an entire year.

Pete worked at a series of jobs after that and eventually lost interest in the idea of teaching school. Before you conclude that I'm being disrespectful by referring to my father as "Pete," I should explain that he hated his real name, Curtis, and wanted people, including his children, to refer to him by his nickname, which was Pete. If I ever refer to him as "Curtis," someone should slap my hand.

At some point in the late twenties, Pete decided to enroll in a business school in Chillicothe, a town in northern Missouri, where he learned a form of magic known as telegraphy. The curriculum was designed with the expectation that the typical student would complete the program in six months. My father was not a typical student. Gifted with exceptional manual dexterity, an eye for detail, and the ability to focus entirely on the task at hand, he learned all there was to learn in three months.

An astonished administrator at the school, noting that nothing like this had ever happened before, said, "There's no point in your staying here another three months. Just forget about the last half of your tuition. You're good enough to get a job right now." With that sincere endorsement, the man sent Pete out into the great world, where he quickly found employment with the Western Union Company.

In the following years, he filled a series of positions in Montana and other western states, cultivated a neatly trimmed mustache, improved his wardrobe, and wrote frequent letters to Jerry, the envelopes of which he addressed with colorful, hand-drawn illustrations, avoiding as much as possible the use of the alphabet. The fact that her name was Hunter undoubtedly made the task easier. This all occurred before the days of bar codes, zip plus four, and shiploads of junk mail; and the Post Office Department delivered these envelopes to Ash Grove, Iowa, with more promptness than anyone would dare hope for today. It was also during this part of his life that he first began working with the dreaded public.

Because Western Union charged by the word, customers tried to keep their telegrams as short as possible. In one such episode that my father recalled, a man was struggling with the sentence "Arrived Butte safely Tuesday."

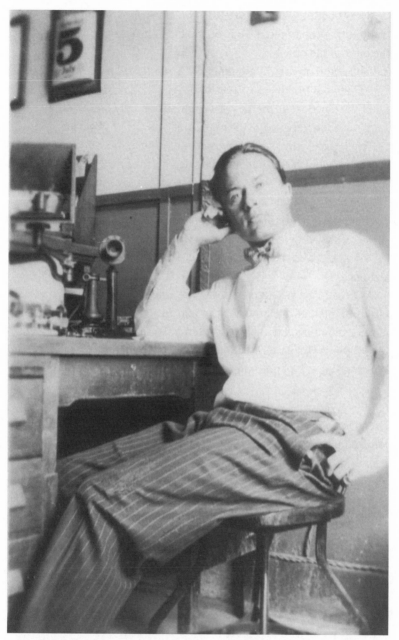

Telegrapher Pete Irelan pauses for a photograph while working at the Western Union office in Chadron, Nebraska, circa 1930. Author's collection.

"How about taking out 'safely'?" the man asked, leaning against the counter that separated the customers from the telegraph equipment at the back of the office.

"You could do that," Pete replied. "It would still make sense."

"What about taking out 'Tuesday'?"

"If the day doesn't matter, you could take it out," Pete said.

"How about 'arrived'?" the man said.

"Well, that's your verb," Pete said, pointing at the word on the piece of paper on which the man had scrawled his message. "It tells what you did. The word 'Butte' all by itself really doesn't say much, does it?"

"Then why not leave in 'arrived' and take out 'Butte'?"

"I suppose if the place isn't important, the word 'arrived' makes sense by itself," Pete said, growing impatient.

"Good. Let's do that," the man said. Then they went on to the second sentence.

As related by my father, the entire discussion with this one man lasted about half an hour. At the end of that time, the man still remained dissatisfied with the cost of his telegram and concluded by saying, "I think I'll just write a letter." By then Pete had a headache and Western Union had nothing to show for his efforts.

———

I don't wish to give the impression that my father despised humanity or longed for unbroken solitude. He never looked for a job as a lighthouse keeper or applied for admission to a monastery. On the contrary, he was outgoing, friendly, and entertaining. He knew that the great majority of people were considerate and polite. But he also learned what all of us must, that there exists a small portion of the human race that lives for the sole purpose of making the rest of us miserable.

If you work for the public, you cannot escape this odious minority. The members of this group will hunt you down, single you out, and make you wish for liberalization of the laws governing the use of blunt instruments. They will ask you the same question ten times, change their minds twenty times, and conclude by saying they don't need your services after all.

These same people will complain about the work you do, regardless of whether you do it right or wrong. They will file grievances with your superiors who work in tall buildings in distant cities, superiors who don't know who you are, what you do, or what, if anything, they should tell you. This inescapable minority will, ultimately, cause you to long for a piece of land back in Iowa, in spite of how infertile, full of gullies, or unproductive it may be — especially if it will bring you closer to a young female schoolteacher with blue eyes, a delicate nose, and a firm chin.

COUNTRY LIVING

My parents were married on Friday, August 19, 1932. This routine statistic becomes more interesting when you consider the setting. One of the local newspapers, the *Davis County Republican*, pointed out in a lengthy article that the couple exchanged vows "before a crowd of several thousand persons in an elaborate public ceremony on the stage in front of the amphitheater at the Davis County Fair." The article goes on to say that the wedding was "the closing feature of the night program" and that "the newlyweds are members of prominent families in the northwest part of Davis County and both are well known."

This well-known couple was "attended by Miss Lily Herteen and Kenneth O. Hunter." Kenneth Hunter was my mother's brother, and Lily Herteen was the woman he would marry two years later, although in 1932 she was about to begin her last year of high school. When Uncle Kenny was ninety-one years old, he remembered that Aunt Lily had given my mother a dress as a wedding present, but he had no recollection of how she could have afforded such a generous gift in the depths of the Great Depression.

To heighten the suspense of the event, the fair board had withheld the names of the happy couple until the last possible moment, and, the *Republican* article continues, "speculation was rife as to whom the principals might be." My father always said that he hadn't even informed his parents, although my mother denied the truth of this claim.

Neither of the "prominent families" had to hire an organist, since "the entire cast of Ernie Young's 'Rainbow Review' provided a colorful setting for the ceremony, and furnished the music for the wedding." Then, in an event my mother had not anticipated, "The bridegroom became the center of attraction immediately after the ceremony when members [female] of the revue swarmed all over him." My mother always admitted that this swarming had infuriated her. My father wisely chose not to comment on his reaction.

Upon hearing of this unusual wedding, one question comes to mind: Why would two members of "prominent families" subject themselves to this strange ceremony? The answer lies in the fact that "prominence" in Davis County, Iowa, during the Depression did not imply wealth. The couple did it for the gifts and the money.

The *Republican* article provides a complete list of the items donated by local merchants. These included such luxuries as a sack of flour from Kline's grocery, a dishpan from the firm of Carroll and Carroll, one pair of overalls from Ray B. Baumgarten, a princess slip from J. H. Taylor, a linen lunch cloth from the Davies Store, and "1 good broom" from the Benner Tea Company. An insurance agency provided a five hundred dollar insurance policy, although my parents owned no property to insure. But best of all, the Davis County Fair Association gave the newlyweds a check for fifty dollars. I don't know what they spent it on, but I'm sure it wasn't a trip to Europe.

With this auspicious ceremony behind them, Pete and Jerry arranged to rent a small farm the next spring from one of my mother's uncles, just a short distance down the road from where my father had grown up. The house was small, but it would easily hold every household item the couple possessed. Having made these plans, they moved in with my father's parents and waited for spring. When the snow began to melt and the creeks began to rise, they combined the money they had managed to save while still single and bought two milk cows and a team of horses. My father preferred to work with mules but couldn't find a suitable team.

In retrospect, one can now see that 1933 was probably the worst year in the history of the United States to begin farming. The price of farm products was low. The cost of production was high. Anyone with a passing acquaintance with arithmetic could calculate that it would have been impossible to make a profit.

If you add to this equation the productivity of the farm my parents had rented, their chances of success appear to have been even less likely. Like most farms in northwest Davis County, this one's scenic value far surpassed its agricultural value. It consisted primarily of high, steep hills unsuitable for cultivation. If you were foolish enough to plow these hills, every hard rain would send your topsoil down the hillside and into the nearest creek, where it would begin its long journey to the Gulf of Mexico.

In an agricultural sense, this terrain was worthless for almost anything but grazing sheep, but my father didn't like sheep because their efficient front teeth protrude at exactly the correct angle to let them

Pete and Gerata Irelan stand amidst the chickens on one of the farms they rented during the 1930s. A long drought and the Great Depression drove them off the farms and into the depots in 1937. Author's collection.

crop off the grass clear to the ground. "If you don't move them from one pasture to another soon enough," he always said, "they'll ruin the pasture they're in." So when spring arrived, Pete bought a few head of Angus calves and hoped they wouldn't break their necks falling down the hills. Those that survived would take two years to grow to market weight. I understand that people who run businesses call this a "cash-flow problem." My father called it "waiting for the eggs to hatch after the hen dies."

On those parts of the farm where the ground was level enough for cultivation, my father grew corn, oats, and hay. Here again, nature worked against him. The soil on the farm, regardless of topography, had never been very fertile, and previous tenants had planted corn year after year, extracting the few nutrients that had once existed. "If I'd looked all over creation," he told me thirty years later, "I couldn't have found a worse farm."

Add to the infertility of the soil the fact that the long drought of 1932 through 1936 had already begun, and the situation looked even worse. The corn and oats were poor, the hay produced only two cuttings, and the calves seemed in no hurry to grow up and ride off to the slaughter-house. Pete sold part of his corn and oats and kept everything else to feed his cattle and horses through the winter. To pay the rent, he had to borrow from the bank, the one misery in life he hated most.

If 1933 was bad, 1934 was a disaster. The hills were still as steep, the soil still as infertile. My mother lost her first child. Then, quite out of nowhere, a disquieting letter arrived from the business school Pete had attended years before in Chillicothe, Missouri.

The essential point of the letter was that my father still owed the school for three months of tuition and that the management would be pleased if he would kindly remit the amount owed and do it quickly. He wrote back to say that an official at the school had assured him that his account was paid in full, owing to the fact that he had completed the course of study in half the time normally required. The school replied by a second letter that my father was very much mistaken because no official had the authority to reduce a student's tuition. The letter went on to state that unless the school received payment, it would have no choice but to initiate legal remedies. Pete chose not to respond.

In the fall, my father sold his beef calves at a small profit, finally bringing some money into the cash-starved operation. My parents sat down at the kitchen table and added up their meager resources.

"What shall we do, Jerry?" my father asked.

"I don't know, Pete." My mother always feared making financial decisions. In actuality, she could make such decisions as well as anyone else, but she lacked self-confidence about these matters.

"We could try it one more year," Pete said. "We could buy some more calves in the spring."

"Yes."

"But we'll have to borrow again."

"I know." She looked at the anxiety in his face, and as always happened at such times, the tears came to her eyes.

They decided to stay one more year.

But 1935 only brought more of what was wrong with 1933 and 1934. The agricultural crisis deepened throughout the Middle West. More and more farmers simply gave up. On some roads, it seemed that every farm had a "For Sale" sign in the front yard.

On July 16, 1935, the business school in Missouri carried through on its threat and filed suit against my father for the unpaid portion of the tuition that he had originally agreed to pay in full. Thanks to the kindness of the present staff in the office of the clerk of court for Davis County, I have obtained photocopies of the files for the entire case and can report these events with faith in their accuracy. On August 23, Donald Harris, the attorney for the school, and W. R. Fimmen, the attorney for my father, argued the case before seven jurors and A. F. Smock, justice of the peace for Drakesville Township.

The evidence and arguments presented were routine and predictable. The location of the trial was far more interesting. The Irelans had lived in Drakesville Township for generations. They got along well with their neighbors and paid their bills as soon as they could. They often made friends and rarely made enemies. At least one of the jurors was a personal friend of my grandfather's.

The trial lasted less than a day. The jury heard the arguments, retired long enough to smoke a cigar, and returned with a verdict in favor of my father. The justice of the peace ordered the plaintiff to pay $16.35 to cover the costs of the case, which included $1.00 apiece for each of the seven jurors. Sensing a local bias in favor of the defendant, the school's lawyer filed an appeal on August 27. The justice of the peace accepted the school's appeal bond of $25.00 and forwarded the case to the district court for eventual retrial.

But for the moment, my parents were in the clear. This victory combined with another piece of good news to lift their spirits even higher: My mother had again become pregnant. Pete and Jerry agreed it was time for a change. First they found a competent doctor in Ottumwa. Then they found a small farm for rent near the village of Troy in the southeast part of Davis County. They made arrangements to move the next spring, after the baby was born.

It seemed to my parents that autumn that better times lay ahead, for neither of them had ever lived on a farm like the one near Troy. It had a large comfortable house. The barn, outbuildings, and fences were in good repair. But best of all, when you walked out into the yard and looked in any direction, all you could see was flat prairie land, with soil as black as an Angus calf.

————

The year 1936 began well for my parents. My sister, Jane, was born by Caesarean section on January 18 at the Ottumwa Hospital. Caesarean babies are always beautiful because their little heads don't suffer the trauma of being forced through the birth canal. My sister and I have always claimed that this also accounts for our extreme good looks as adults. Other observers have disputed all aspects of this claim.

When spring arrived my parents and their baby moved to the farm near Troy. Pete planted a large field of corn and sowed a field of timothy. He bought a few more Angus calves and put them out to pasture. Together, he and my mother planted a large garden. It seldom rained, but everything else seemed to be going well.

Then the rain stopped entirely.

From that point on, 1936 descended into a catastrophe of Biblical proportions. The drought in southern Iowa reached its peak. It simply did not rain. It didn't even sprinkle. For weeks at a time, the temperature rose to levels that killed the old and infirm. A hot, dry wind blew continually, whipping the dust into huge clouds. For some unfortunate reason, the county chose just that summer to gravel the road that passed by the house, thereby adding the dust of crushed limestone to the dust from the topsoil. The baby grew ill from the heat and the dust. My parents hung wet sheets over the doors and windows in an attempt to keep the dust out.

The garden withered in the drought. Just when it seemed that nothing more could go wrong, swarms of grasshoppers and chinch bugs moved in from the south. They descended on the cornfield and stripped it down to the bare stalks. Simultaneously, they attacked the garden, leaving nothing but eggplant. Eggplant, along with milk from the two cows, provided the only food my parents ate for months. The Angus calves were still in the pasture, but were far too valuable to slaughter for personal use.

"I got so sick of eggplant that summer," my mother often said, "that I swore I would never eat it again." I can personally testify that she did not break that vow. During my entire childhood, eggplant remained as foreign to me as the ziggurats of Babylonia. I never even saw an eggplant until the age of twenty-six, and when I finally did see one I had to ask somebody what it was. I try to remain open-minded about anything new to me, but I have to admit that I found no beauty in that eggplant.

Finally, with the early symptoms of malnutrition starting to appear, most noticeably in my mother, who was nursing a baby, word came that the WPA was hiring men to build a state park near Keosauqua, twelve miles to the east. Pete immediately signed on. My parents owned a car, but because they had no money for gasoline, my father rose at four o'clock each morning, milked the cows, and walked to Keosauqua. Then he walked back in the evening, arriving home about eight, when he milked the cows again.

The men were paid in surplus oats and wheat, which my father later told me "was the best pay I ever received." The grain, which the men received in generous amounts, quickly improved the diets of both humans and livestock. The cattle and horses enjoyed the oats. My parents took the wheat to a mill and gratefully added bread to their meals of milk and eggplant. I have heard people claim that President Roosevelt's New Deal programs, such as the WPA, did little to improve the lives of working people during the Great Depression. I invite those critics to eat nothing but milk and eggplant for a few months.

While my father worked on the park at Keosauqua, Uncle Kenny found employment in a similar project at Lake Wapello State Park in western Davis County. Like my father, he couldn't afford gasoline for the car. "I spent more time walking than working," he told me. Nonetheless, the WPA paid him fifty cents a day, and that park, built by desperately poor men, is now one of the most beautiful places in the area. And in the year 2000, at the age of ninety-one, Uncle Kenny watched his grandson Justin marry a lovely blond-haired girl on a promontory of that lake.

But back in 1936, for reasons unknown to me, the grasshoppers and chinch bugs had ignored my father's timothy, which continued to grow despite the drought. One Saturday the landlord, "a man advanced in years" as my mother described him, came to the door and asked my father when he intended to mow the timothy for hay.

"I'm not going to mow it for hay," Pete said.

"Why not?" asked the landlord.

My father knew that timothy seed was one of the only farm commodities bringing a good price that year. "I'm going to let it go to seed and have it thrashed out," he said.

I don't know why, but this announcement infuriated the landlord. Perhaps he feared that a storm might ruin the field and my parents wouldn't be able to pay the rent. In any event, he literally shouted, "I want that field cut now!"

"We didn't say anything originally about cutting it for hay," Pete said. "I'm letting it go to seed."

The landlord finally left, still just as angry as before, but according to my mother, he came back several times to renew his demands. "He'd just cuss Pete out," she said, "but Pete paid no attention to him. He'd just look away as if no one was there."

After the timothy had matured, Pete cut it by hand, tied it into sheaves, and stacked it in shocks to cure. When the neighborhood thrashing machine arrived at the farm, the timothy produced a marvelous yield — "bushels and bushels of seed," my mother said. My parents sold it at an excellent price. That fall, when they added up their gains and losses, they discovered something remarkable: In a year in which one disaster had followed another on the parched little farm, and although they were still in debt from the past, 1936 was the first year in which they made a profit.

THE CB&Q

The landlord of the farm near Troy did not invite my parents back for a second year. Perhaps he held some residual misgivings about the issue of the timothy field. Perhaps he intended to open Troy's first drive-in movie theater and project the flickering image of Hollywood's latest masterpiece off the side of the barn. In any event, he informed my parents quite explicitly that they would have to vacate the premises by March 1, 1937, the first of March being the traditional moving day among farmers in the Middle West. By that date the roads would be passable for horses and wagons, and by sometime in April one might hope to begin preparing the soil for the new growing season. My parents rented an eighty-acre farm two miles north of Bloomfield and prayed for more rain and fewer insects.

On moving day, my parents bundled up their one-year-old baby and hauled their possessions to the new farm. Because I would later spend sixteen years of my life on that farm, I could describe it in intimate detail. But I will resist that temptation for the present and say only that I have never seen anywhere on God's earth an eighty-acre farm more worthless than that one.

On April 20 of that same year, all parties involved assembled at the Davis County Courthouse for retrial of the case between the business school in Chillicothe, Missouri, and C. G. Irelan. The courthouse stands on a green lawn in the center of Bloomfield's town square. The county erected the building in 1877 in the Second Empire style, with a limestone façade, a mansard roof shingled with dark-gray slate, and a tall clock tower to which the eye is inevitably drawn. At the peak of the clock tower stands a statue of Justitia, Goddess of Justice, facing east toward Rome.

In the high-ceilinged courtroom, the judge's bench, the jury box, the railing, the seats for spectators, and all the other wooden furnishings gleam with the uniform dark hue of native walnut. Tall narrow windows on the west side admit a flood of natural light. Regrettably, the decisions concerning life, death, property, and money rendered in this room have given the individuals involved little motivation to consider these surroundings.

The same lawyers from the first trial argued the case before District Court Judge R. W. Smith. As with the initial trial, the retrial lasted less than a day. Neither side disputed the facts of the case, which were simple and straightforward. Donald Harris, the lawyer for the school, pointed out that my father had signed a contract to pay for six months of tuition but that he had paid for only three months. The fact that he had mastered the art of telegraphy in record time and had left the school three months early, Mr. Harris argued, did not release him from his contractual obligation to pay for the entire six months of tuition.

W. R. Fimmen, my father's lawyer, argued eloquently that Mr. Irelan should not have to pay for what he had not received, especially given the acknowledged fact that an authorized agent of the school had told him that he need not pay the last three months of tuition. This oral agreement, according to Mr. Fimmen, abrogated the terms of the written contract. He noted that the school had not helped the defendant find employment, even though the contract had stated that it would. Likewise, he said that the school had not provided meals to the defendant for the full six months, although that, too, had been promised in the contract.

Finally, he pointed out with a touch of irony that the plaintiff, instead of suing the defendant, should be paying him for permission to give his name to prospective students as an example of a former student who had received such excellent training that he had completed the program three months early and immediately acquired a job without help or referrals from anyone.

In his decision, while expressing sympathy for my father's situation, Judge Smith stated that in this case both the evidence and the letter of the law were far too clear to allow for anything but a ruling in favor of the plaintiff. A signed contract was a signed contract. Like almost everyone else in the room, the judge knew my father personally. With considerable embarrassment, he instructed the defendant to pay $93.26 for the judgment, interest, and costs in full.

The court adjourned, the judge made a hasty exit, Mr. Fimmen expressed his regrets at the outcome of the trial, and Mr. Harris walked over to say, "I hope there's no hard feelings about this, Pete."

"Don't give it another thought, Don. It's my own fault for not getting something in writing from those people." Then Mr. Harris walked away, and my father stood there contemplating a fact every bit as clear as the contract he had signed with the school many years before: He did not have $93.26.

As he considered this fact, one of the few strangers in the courtroom walked up and introduced himself. My mother recalled that he was a tall man, neatly dressed in a dark-gray suit and a blue tie. The business school had sent him to observe the trial and he wondered if he might have a few moments of my father's time.

"You can have all day," Pete said. "Then I'll have to go home and milk the cows."

"I know these are tough times," the man said, looking down at the hat in his hands, "especially for farmers."

"And they just got a lot tougher," Pete said.

"You know, the railroads are looking for telegraphers," the man said, now peering directly at my father's face. "Would you be interested if I could find you a job?"

Pete's spirits suddenly rose. "Yes," he said without hesitation. He was never a man to waste time making decisions.

"Where would you be willing to go?"

"Anywhere."

"I'll see what I can do," the man said. "It could take me a while to find the right job, but I promise you that I will find one."

"Take as long as you need," Pete said. "I'll still be here." The man shook hands, smiled for the first time, and walked away.

My parents had no illusions about the motivations of the man from the school. He knew that Pete had no money and wanted him to get a job so that he could pay the judgment. And, in fact, given the likelihood that Pete would soon find a position with a railroad, one of the banks in Bloomfield gave him a loan, and on April 29, 1937, he wrote a check in the amount of $93.26 to the clerk of the district court for Davis County, Iowa, thereby relieving himself of any further obligation in the matter of case number 8952, docket 33, page 159. The original receipt, at which I am presently looking, appears to have been properly completed and signed by W. R. McMains, clerk of court. The school got its money. I don't know whether the place still exists, and I have no plans to drive down to Missouri to find out.

One day in the spring of 1937, something unexpected happened. It began to rain. It rained day after day in the manner that every farmer loves, so gently that it soaks the ground without washing away even a particle of topsoil. It rained on the new state parks built by the WPA, on the hills where sheep grazed contentedly, and on the large field of oats my father had sown by hand, using the same rhythm and motions farmers have used for six thousand years.

On a hot summer afternoon that same year, my mother walked down the farm lane to the mailbox. Along with the usual bills, she found a letter addressed to Mr. C. G. Irelan. But what she found more interesting was the return address:

> C.B.&Q. R.R. Co.
> Burlington Building
> 547 W. Jackson Blvd.
> Chicago, Ill.

The "C.B.&Q. R.R. Co." was the Chicago, Burlington & Quincy Railroad Company, more commonly known as the Burlington Railroad or simply the CB&Q. By the end of the twentieth century, the CB&Q had merged with the Great Northern and the Santa Fe to form the mammoth Burlington Northern Santa Fe Railroad. But in 1937 it was still just the CB&Q, and my mother knew exactly what those letters stood for.

She also knew what the envelope contained and that my father would not mind if she opened it, which she proceeded to do. The letter she found inside invited my father to report to the Burlington Station in Lincoln, Nebraska, where he would receive the training needed to become a depot agent. Along with the letter, she found a passenger ticket for the trip from Ottumwa to Lincoln.

Mother walked out to the field north of the house where my father was stacking oat straw on a wagon. She showed him the letter, and his interest in oat straw suddenly plummeted. Resisting the urge to drive immediately to Ottumwa to catch the next westbound train, he finished loading the wagon, unloaded it at the barn, and turned the horses out to pasture. He made what arrangements he could with the landlady; left the two milk cows in the care of my mother, who could milk a cow faster than he could anyway; and three days after receiving the letter from Chicago, dressed in his best suit, he stepped off the train at the CB&Q Station in Lincoln.

After an introductory visit to the station, he rented a nearby sleeping room that met his requirements for cost, size, furnishings, and relative lack of vermin. The next morning, he went to work. In the following four months, he learned everything he would ever need to know about railroads: how to interpret the concise telegrams from the dispatcher, how to type a train order giving a train crew any instructions needed, how to attach two identical orders to two train-order hoops, how to hold the first of these up at the precise height and angle for the engineer and then hold up the second one for the conductor, both of whom were riding on a train that might be moving slowly or at speeds up to seventy or eighty miles per hour. On well-maintained track and with certain speed-loving engineers at the throttle, the train could be going even faster.

Pete also learned how to watch every train that passed for hotboxes (overheated axle bearings) or other mechanical failures that could send it into a deadly tangle of cars and humans. He learned how to signal an engineer with flag or lantern and how to interpret the engineer's responding whistle. He learned how to decode signal lights along the tracks, how to write freight orders for shipments of any size, and how to find his way through a maze of timetables in order to get a passenger from Lincoln, Nebraska, to Bangor, Maine, via the most direct route. And on behalf of the United States Post Office, he learned how to handle mailbags with regard for neither rain nor snow nor sleet nor dark of night.

In short, he had to learn and remember more than I could ever list or recall, including, finally, how to keep the depot clean and tidy. This has to have been the last lesson taught and the first ignored, for never in my life have I seen a small-town depot that was clean and tidy, although my mother worked in a succession of depots until I was two years old, and I'm sure that hers were spotless.

Finally, on November 1, 1937, Pete received a letter from Mr. C. N. Miller. In typical railroad prose, brief and to the point, Mr. Miller wrote:

> Looks like we will have a custodianship at Murphy for the winter and wondered if you would be interested in taking it. The position pays $35.00 per month and living rooms are provided in the depot.

While located there you will have opportunity to go to adjoining stations and post yourself on station and train order work and be posted to go out in the spring.

A number of details in this letter may require explanation. First of all, "custodianship" has nothing to do with janitorial work. It refers to the management of a depot in a town so small that anyone could handle the job with almost no training, someone, for example, exactly like my mother, for whom the "living rooms" would be a special enticement. The enticement for my father would be the "station and train order work" at larger depots, which would pay considerably more than the job at Murphy. Then, in the spring, my mother would become a CB&Q employee as the custodian at Murphy, and my father would be sent wherever needed in that region, a standard procedure for agents with the least seniority.

In case this discussion of the custodianship at Murphy has aroused your curiosity about the location of that town, I should warn you that it does not appear on most recent road maps of Nebraska. Even a telephone call to the Nebraska Tourism Office left me with no clue to the whereabouts of Murphy. The polite young man with whom I spoke found the town of Murray for me, but I had to confess that I had no interest in Murray. I was about to visit the map room in the library of a nearby university, when I stumbled upon exactly the map I needed at a gas station one block from where I live. Murphy stands just off Route 34 approximately six miles west of Highway 14 in the southern half of the state.

I never doubted the existence of Murphy, regardless of what the road maps indicated, for I had my mother's testimony that it existed in 1937. According to her account, Murphy contained, in addition to the depot, a grain elevator, a functioning grocery store, and several small frame houses. She knew the town well, because as soon as Mr. Miller offered my father the position at Murphy, Pete immediately accepted it and caught the next train back to Iowa, where he sold his horses and livestock, gave the landlady all the straw and grain in lieu of cash rent, bought a small trailer and hitched it to the car, loaded it with all the household possessions he and my mother owned, and took off for Murphy.

When they reached Lincoln, my mother sent my grandmother a postcard bearing a picture of the Burlington Station where Pete had learned the railroad business, a long three-story building constructed of red brick and limestone. On the card, she wrote

Dear Mother,

Got into Lincoln about 6:30. Just now finished eating a bite of warm supper. Everything OK so far. Will go on as far as Tamora tonight, then finish the drive tomorrow. Will be farther than I had said when we get there. Baby slept all afternoon.

Love, G. H. I.

THIRTEEN MEN

One fall while my parents and sister were living in the CB&Q depot in Murphy, an early blizzard swept across the Great Plains, driving all but the foolish or unlucky indoors. The sound of a freight train taking on corn at the grain elevator woke my father late one night. Murphy stood on the main line, so this was a common occurrence. Trains stopped or sped past at all hours of the day or night. Pete went back to sleep as the train pulled away.

But another sound soon woke him again. Someone was knocking at the waiting-room door, which was definitely not a common occurrence in little Murphy at that hour. My father put on his clothes, woke my mother, and told her what was happening. Then he walked out of the living quarters, through the office, and across the waiting room to see who could have business to transact at that unlikely hour.

He stopped at the door and looked out the window. In the glare from the light above the brick platform, he saw a group of men huddled together against the cold. The bravest of the lot, a black man, stood near the door while the others kept their distance. From the way they were dressed, my father instantly realized what kind of men they were and how they had come to be there. They all wore overalls, work shoes, short heavy coats, thick cloth gloves, and winter caps with the flaps turned down to protect their ears. Pete turned on the waiting-room light, unlocked the door, and swung it open.

"What are you fellows doing out here in this cold?" he asked the black man. He already knew the answer, but it would have been rude to show that he knew.

"The conductor put us off the train," the man said.

"How many of you are there?" Pete asked.

"There's eleven here and two more down there trying to get into a boxcar," the man said, pointing at a boxcar sitting on a sidetrack.

"Oh, somebody better tell them not to do that," Pete said. "That car is sealed to go out in the morning. They could get in trouble doing that. Get everybody to come back here and I'll build up the fire in the waiting room." The seal he referred to was nothing more than a strip of paper printed with dire warnings and attached to both the door and the body of the boxcar. To open the door, you had to break the seal. Anyone could break it, but to do so without permission was against the law and could result in a prison sentence.

The man ran back to the group on the platform, and a few of them ran to get the other two before they, in their innocence, violated a federal law. All thirteen soon crowded into the waiting room, where Pete was shaking down the spent ashes in the coal stove. "Find a place to lie down," he said. "I'll get this fire going and you can get some sleep." The men quickly accepted his invitation and lay down on the bare wooden floor wherever they could. Most of them were white. A few were black. The Great Depression excluded no one on the basis of race. "Where you fellows been?" Pete said after adding more coal and closing the door of the stove.

"We were working in the beet fields," one of the men said, referring to sugar beets, "but the blizzard ruined the crop and they put us out."

"Without pay," another man said with a touch of resentment.

"Where you from?" Pete said. The men told him. All were from farms and towns in Iowa, Missouri, and Illinois. Like millions of other desperate men during the Depression, they had left their families in search of work. Any kind of work. Now they were trying to get back home with little or no money to show for their trouble.

The fire in the stove heated up, and Pete set the draft for the night. By then the men were snoring peacefully. He left as quietly as he could, and soon he, my mother, and little Janey were sleeping, too.

———

My parents awoke early the next morning, as they always did. Pete got dressed and walked out of the bedroom and through the small parlor to the office, which also served as the kitchen. Many people would have found these quarters too small and too simple, but my parents never complained. They paid no rent, and the railroad provided coal, electricity, and water without charge. My mother and father felt lucky to have jobs when so many other people couldn't find one.

Pete looked out the ticket window at the thirteen men, all of whom were still sleeping soundly. After building up the fire in the office stove, he slipped out by way of the freight room and walked through the snow to the grocery store, where he bought a pound of ground coffee and a few loaves of bread. Meanwhile, my mother opened two of the half-gallon jars of beef that she had canned before leaving Iowa.

My father returned, and as the men began to stir, Pete brewed the coffee and Jerry heated up the beef. By the time my father got a good fire going in the waiting-room stove, my mother was ready to dispense coffee and sandwiches through the ticket window to anybody who wanted them. It will come as no surprise that every man wanted both coffee and sandwiches and that they gladly accepted my mother's invitation to come back for more if they wanted it.

One man put a quarter on the ledge of the ticket window. "What's that for?" my mother said, pretending not to understand the purpose of quarters.

"It's for my sandwiches," the man said. "I'd pay more if I had it."

"We don't want any money," Mother said. "You'd better hold on to that. You'll need it before you get back home." The man reluctantly took back the quarter.

Another man asked my father for a broom. "A broom?" Pete said.

"Yes," the man said. "Some of us were smoking last night, and I want to sweep up the ashes."

Pete looked at the floor. There were no ashes. But he understood. The man was a worker, and he wanted to do something. My father gave him a broom, and he swept the entire floor, managing to collect a small quantity of dust.

Finally, Pete had to ask the embarrassing question he had avoided until then: "How do you men plan to get out of town?"

"We'd like to go out on the local if we can," one of them said, referring to the next freight train that would stop in a town as small as Murphy.

"All right," Pete said. "There'll be one along shortly. When it gets here, why don't you just stay inside while I go out to talk to the conductor."

The train arrived half an hour later. After the crew had maneuvered the boxcar from the siding into the correct part of the train, according to its destination, and after the brakeman had attached the hoses, the conductor headed for the depot as he normally did. Little Jane usually ran out to meet him, but this time Pete went out instead.

The temperature had dropped overnight, and the wind blew even harder. Snowdrifts grew behind any object that broke the uniform flatness of the plains. After exchanging greetings with the conductor, Pete said, "There are thirteen men in the waiting room. They were harvesting beets but were let go without pay when the storm ruined the crop. The conductor put them off the local last night with no money and no place to go. If I hadn't let them in the waiting room, they would've broken in somewhere or frozen to death, and the railroad would've had to take the blame."

The conductor looked around the tiny town with obvious comprehension of my father's point. "What do you think we should do, Pete?" he said.

"Why don't you go around on the other side of the train where you can't see what's happening," Pete said, "and I'll tell them to climb into an empty boxcar and close the doors. After the train leaves, I'll wire Lincoln and tell them what I've done. If they don't like it, I'm the one who'll have to answer for it."

"Okay," the conductor said. "I think you're right. We can't let them freeze, and we can't keep them here all winter. If Lincoln gives you a lot of guff, you can tell them I went along with it." With that said, he walked around to the other side of the train and stared into the distance while my father went back into the depot, where he quickly told the men what to do.

"Not one of them left without saying 'Thank you,'" my mother remembered years later. "I know they meant it, and I always wondered if all of them got home safely."

As the train pulled away, Pete wired Lincoln and related what had happened and what he had done. Then he asked that all conductors be instructed not to put any more men off the trains in Murphy. "My wife and daughter are usually here alone. The sheriff is miles away. These were good men. The next bunch might not be."

The conductors ordered no more men off the trains at Murphy. Pete never received a word of criticism from the railroad. I heard this story dozens of times from both my parents as I was growing up. Whenever my mother concluded the tale, she would say, "I don't know what the company thought by putting them out that way." She didn't blame the conductor. He was a fellow worker. She blamed the company. The company made the rules and the conductors had to enforce them, although sometimes one of them could be induced to avert his eyes and gaze across the frozen whiteness of the plains.

GREAT PLAINS

My mother blossomed in Nebraska, like a wildflower beneath the vaulting blue sky of the Great Plains. She loved it there, not because of wealth, position, or power, none of which she possessed, but because she was out among the people — working, caring for her child, living in places unlike any she had lived in before. Altogether, she, my father, and my sister lived in Nebraska about five years: first in Murphy, then in Pauline, where they again lived in the depot, and finally in Milford, where, because the depot had no living quarters, they rented a small but adequate house. I'm happy to report that, unlike Murphy, I've had no trouble finding both Pauline and Milford on every map of Nebraska I've seen.

While living in these little towns, my mother and sister took occasional trips to Iowa to visit my grandparents, who by then had moved into Ottumwa, leaving the house and farm in the energetic care of Uncle Kenny and Aunt Lily. Usually, Mother and my sister traveled by train. As an employee of the CB&Q, my mother could travel anywhere on that railroad, along with my sister, at no charge. And because all the train crews knew them, they received preferential treatment.

The porters, all of whom were black men, always carried little Jane to her seat, while the conductors or brakemen, all of whom were white men, carried the luggage. I have often wondered if the porters of that era were required to pass examinations certifying their affection for small children. Normally, the porters carried the luggage, but when young children appeared, the porters left the heavy lifting for the conductors and brakemen.

On one occasion, for reasons never explained to me, my mother and sister drove to Iowa and back to Nebraska. After crossing the state line, which is defined by the Missouri River, two highway patrolmen, with red lights flashing, motioned for Mother to stop.

"Sorry, ma'am," one of them said with official politeness, "but we'll have to search your car."

"Search the car?" Mother said, baffled by this strange demand.

"Yes, ma'am. We have to search the car." And they proceeded to do so.

After the search, during which they found two suitcases, a spare tire, a bumper jack, a wheel wrench, and a teddy bear, they apologized for the inconvenience.

"Now do you mind telling me why you did this?" my mother said, still confused and becoming increasingly angry.

"We're looking for bootleggers," one of the patrolmen said. National prohibition had ended in 1933, but bootlegging was, and still is, a crime.

"Bootleggers?" Mother said, her anger reaching new heights. "You thought a lone woman and a little child were bootleggers?" The patrolmen had no way of knowing it, but my mother came from a long line of teetotalers. Nothing the man could have said would have insulted her more, and despite her religious and forgiving nature, she possessed a volatile temper. "Where," she said, "would you get an idea like that?"

Now on the defensive in the face of a superior intellect and justifiable resentment, the patrolmen again mumbled their apologies. Then one of them tried to explain. "You see, ma'am, the bootleggers don't just send a man with a truck across the state line anymore. They know we'd stop him and search the truck. So they've started sending people you generally wouldn't suspect, people like you. So now we stop people who look the most innocent. We're very sorry."

Somewhat placated, my mother let the matter rest and drove on. But the next time, she took the train.

In all honesty, it must be admitted that sometimes my mother would do things that, in retrospect, even she had to confess were foolhardy. While living in Pauline, she and Jane took the train to Ottumwa for Christmas, as they did every year. As they were riding back to Nebraska early in January, the snow stopped, the wind rose, and the temperature began to fall. Pauline stood on a spur south of the main line of the CB&Q, and the passenger trains didn't go there. The closest stop was at Hastings, which meant that Mother and Jane would have to drive from the depot in Hastings to the depot in Pauline, a distance of about fifteen miles.

As the train approached Hastings in the dark of night, the conductor stopped at the seats where Mother was sitting and Jane was sleeping.

"Mrs. Irelan," he said, "the weather has turned terribly cold since you left Ottumwa. You'd better not plan to drive back to Pauline tonight."

"Oh, I have to get back tonight," Mother said.

"Surely there's nothing in Pauline that can't wait until tomorrow," he said.

"No, I have to go tonight," she said, her stubbornness now augmenting her poor judgment.

"I'll talk to the agent when we get to Hastings," the conductor said and quickly walked away before Mother could turn his sensible advice into an argument — argument being a skill at which she excelled.

Just as the train reached Hastings, two porters suddenly appeared at my mother's side. In accordance with a conspiracy they and the conductor had planned, one man grabbed Jane, the other grabbed the luggage, and they rushed off the train and into the depot where my mother would have to follow. As she walked across the station platform, she saw the conductor speaking rapidly to the depot agent, who nodded his head to indicate both his understanding and agreement.

The porters said good-bye to Jane and my mother, then ran back to the train. Passengers hurried off and others hurried on. Mailbags flew from the mail car as others flew in. A porter grabbed the Pullman stool and climbed the steps of the coach. The conductor looked at his pocket watch, signaled the highball with his lantern, waited for the responding whistle from the engineer, and stepped aboard at the exact moment that the train started to move. Minutes later, the train, one of the many silver-colored Burlington Zephyrs, a city unto itself, disappeared into the night.

Back in the depot office, while Jane drooped sleepily in a wooden swivel chair, my mother was again engaged in earnest debate, this time with the depot agent. "You can't go back tonight," he said.

"I have to," she said.

"There won't be another car on the road. If your car breaks down, there won't be anyone to help you and you'll freeze to death before morning." The agent was not exaggerating. Autos in the 1930s weren't as reliable as they are now, and even today, anyone in Nebraska should think carefully before driving off on a night like that one.

"I have to get back," Mother insisted.

"There's a nice little room with a cot in back. You and Jane can curl up in there, sleep all night, and drive back in the morning."

"No, I'd better go now."

"Pete's in Grand Island. No one expects you in Pauline tonight. No one needs you, and even if they did, they could wait until morning."

By my mother's own account, this debate continued for some time. The more reasonable the agent became, the more unreasonable she became. Finally, he gave up. More trains, more passengers, and more mailbags would soon arrive. He went out to my parents' car and looked at the tires. He checked the radiator, the battery cables, the spark plug wires, the hoses, the belts, and anything else he could see. Finally, he started the car to warm it up and checked the gas gauge and the lights. Then he went back into the depot, carried the bags out, and put them into the trunk while Mother carried Jane out and laid her on the backseat, where she curled up and went back to sleep.

After Mother had driven out of Hastings and started toward Pauline, the true seriousness of her situation finally hit her. The temperature had fallen well below zero. The wind blew so hard that she had to grip the wheel to avoid losing control of the car. Wind-driven snow flew across the road in waves, obscuring her vision, forcing her to drive no faster than ten or fifteen miles per hour. She considered going back to Hastings, but couldn't see well enough to turn around.

"I didn't meet a single car," she told me. "I got scared. I don't know a thing about cars and can't imagine what I would've done if I'd had trouble."

But after what seemed to her like hours, Pauline came into view, and as she drove up to the depot she was surprised to see that the lights were on. Once inside, she found that the fire in the office stove was burning warmly and that one of the section men was sitting comfortably beside it, dressed in the same overalls he might have worn while repairing the track. "Pretty cold out there tonight, isn't it?" he said. Then he grinned broadly at his own understatement.

My mother told me that she was never happier to see a section man in her entire life. He belonged to a race of men known for their love of storytelling and their hard physical work. Each crew of these men maintained a specific section of track, which is why they were called "section men." And now this section man had another story he could tell and retell until the day he died, a story about the night that a depot agent in Hastings had called him at his house in Pauline to say that Mrs. Irelan and her little girl had driven off on a bitterly cold night and that someone had better go down to the depot, start a fire in the stove, and make sure she got there within a reasonable period of time. And if she didn't, someone had better go out looking for her.

"It was the stupidest thing I ever did," my mother always said. "I don't know what I was thinking. Thank God, there were people with good sense looking out for me."

But despite conditions that were far from ideal — blizzards, meager wages, cramped living quarters, dust storms worse than those in Iowa, and the frequent absence of her husband — my mother thrived in Nebraska. Decades later, she told my sister that her five years on the Great Plains were the happiest in her life.

————

For my father, life on the plains was not quite as happy. He couldn't leave a little depot like the one in Pauline in the care of someone else and visit his relatives in Iowa as my mother could. Instead, he repeatedly had to say good-bye to his wife and child and go off to some busy station that desperately needed his skills. His life assumed a pattern of endless work interrupted by endless travel. Moreover, he had to work whatever eight-hour trick, or shift, was needed. First trick lasted from eight in the morning until four in the afternoon. Second trick lasted from four until midnight. And third trick ran from midnight until eight in the morning.

As an example of his work schedule, consider the first two weeks of January in 1940. During that period, Pete worked at Baird (third trick), Fremont (third), Oreapolis (second), Ravenna (first), and Lincoln (first). The fact that he rode the trains deadhead from one depot to another — meaning that he was paid while traveling, although at a lower rate than usual — did little to relieve the sleep deprivation that this irregular schedule caused. During one five-day period in March of 1940, he worked in four different depots on two different tricks, first and second. The rate of pay differed from depot to depot. On these five days, the highest rate was seventy-five cents per hour and the lowest rate was sixty-four cents per hour. After returning to Iowa in 1941, in one two-week period during the last half of April, he worked in Mount Pleasant, Ottumwa, Birmingham, Ottumwa again, Lawler, Birmingham again, Lockridge, Ottumwa for the third time, and Mount Pleasant again. It will come as no surprise that he worked all three tricks during these two weeks.

The hourly pay that he received at any depot or while riding dead-head did not reflect the inherent generosity of the railroad. It reflected, instead, decades of union negotiations between the Order of Railroad Telegraphers and the CB&Q. As in any other industry, the company offered as little as it could hope to pay and the union demanded as much as it could hope to receive. When negotiations failed, strikes followed. As my mother reminded me at least once a week throughout my entire childhood, "Without unions, the working people would have nothing."

The reader might reasonably ask at this point how I could possibly know my father's work schedule and hourly pay during those years just mentioned, all of which passed before I was born. The answer is quite simple. Pete kept meticulous records, in eight small bound notebooks, for every day that he worked from 1937 to 1966. I have found six of these notebooks and would trade the small toe of my left foot if I could find the other two. In these notebooks, he recorded the date, the depot he worked in, the trick he worked, the number of hours he worked, and his hourly rate of pay. He also kept records for my mother in these note-books, although they were much simpler, given that she didn't have to travel from one depot to another every time the wind shifted.

The reason my father kept such detailed records is that the railroad's bookkeepers didn't always receive the correct information they needed to accurately compute his earnings for each two-week pay period. I'm sure that most other agents recorded the same sort of information. Because Pete kept good records, he could then send in the information the bookkeepers needed to correct the error. He always recorded these corrections as "Back Pay" in his notebooks. My father did not distrust the bookkeepers or the company officials. He didn't suspect, for example, that the CB&Q would deliberately try to cheat him out of the sixty-five cents per hour that he earned for eight hours of work at Farwell, Nebraska, on October 4, 1938. But although it pains me to reveal it, the mighty Burlington Railroad did sometimes make mistakes.

Occasionally, my mother would leave her little depot at Murphy or Pauline or Milford in the care of another Burlington employee, and she and Jane would join Pete in his travels. Jane has faint memories of these travels — seeing a tall building in Lincoln, looking down from a high place in or near Cheyenne, Wyoming, repeatedly falling asleep on trains to somewhere. The presence of his wife and child did not make Pete's schedule any less exhausting, but he always found in them immediate sympathy and consolation. For Mother and Jane, the cheap

Pete Irelan and his daughter, Jane, stand on a Chicago, Burlington & Quincy depot platform on the Great Plains, somewhere in Nebraska, sometime in the late 1930s. Author's collection.

hotels, the small cafés, and the frequent train rides offered a continual adventure, an adventure that had only just begun. For by then, my family had transformed itself into what it would remain for thirty years: a family that lived in accordance with timetables, freight rates, ticket prices, train orders, union contracts, the constant rattle of the telegraph, luxury express trains bound for the coast, and the supreme master of all things that moved by rail, time — time as measured by my father's gold pocket watch, the Hamilton Railway Special — Central Standard Time.

TRAMPS

In recent years, a great deal of ink, film, and videotape has been used to document a dying breed of men known as tramps or hobos. Unlike the thirteen migrant workers my parents befriended during the Depression, tramps did not ride the freight trains in search of work. They rode the freights to avoid work. Defenders of these men have made fine distinctions between hobos and tramps. According to these accounts, hobos would work for a meal, then move on. Tramps would merely ask for food without offering any work in return. Those who sympathize with these men have described them as romantic loners, men unable to settle down and conform to the restrictions of a stultifying pecuniary society. There is even an annual hobo convention somewhere in Iowa, although cynics may argue that holding a convention for romantic loners is inherently contradictory.

Despite my mother's generous disposition, she did not share this romantic notion of these men, regardless of what you called them. When Mother assumed the custodianship at the depot in Murphy, CB&Q officials in Lincoln warned her never to give food to tramps. "If you give food to one," they said, "you'll soon have a steady stream of them coming to the door."

Conductors, brakemen, engineers, dispatchers, and section men all repeated this advice. "Some of these men aren't quite right in the head," a conductor told her. "I don't think many of them are dangerous, but you never know."

It didn't take a great deal of this advice to convince my mother of its wisdom. She and my father did not earn all that much money, and she didn't have a lot of food to give away. Moreover, she came from a large family of people who had always worked for a living, and she didn't see why able-bodied men couldn't work for theirs.

When she was a child growing up on the farm, tramps had sometimes stopped to ask for food. They were polite and deferential, and my grandmother usually gave them something. But these occasional visitors to an isolated farm in no way compared to the large number of tramps who traveled the main line of the CB&Q. Every day at least one would come to the depot, walk through the waiting room, and stop at the ticket window. By his appearance, Mother knew that he hadn't come to buy a ticket for the *California Zephyr*. The *California Zephyr* didn't stop at Murphy anyway, but the point is no less valid.

"I wondered if you could spare a bite to eat," the man would say.

"No, sorry," Mother said.

"Nothing at all?"

"No, I'm afraid not." Then she would wave her hand in a gesture of dismissal. This usually convinced the tramp, and he went on his way, no doubt hoping for better luck at the next house or depot.

Sometimes the man would look around in a vaguely threatening way, as if trying to see who else was there. In fact, no one else but little Janey was there. Pete was almost always working at a station in a larger town many miles away. Mother began keeping the door to the office locked at all times. "I never gave any of them a thing to eat," she told me, "even though I felt guilty about it with the ones who looked so forlorn. But I knew I couldn't feed everyone who came through the door."

On the rare occasions when my father was in Murphy, he went to the ticket window when a tramp appeared and quickly advised him that he couldn't give him a thing. That's all it took. The man went on his way. The tramps seemed to think that they might be able to talk a woman into giving them something to eat, but that a man could not be persuaded.

One warm spring day when Pete was not in Murphy, a tramp came to the ticket window and said, "How about something to eat?"

"No, sorry," Mother said.

"Come on, just a little something."

"No, I don't have anything to give you."

"I know better than that," the man said, his voice rising. "I know plenty of men who got a good meal here."

"Not from me, they didn't." Mother began to get frightened.

"Oh, don't give me that," the man shouted.

"I don't have a thing for you," Mother said, her voice rising. "You might as well go on your way."

"I'm not leaving until I get something to eat." Jane stood beside her mother, looking up at the loud man, who began stomping around the waiting room like a spoiled child.

Mother took this opportunity to go to the phone and call the grocery store, the only store and the only gathering place in tiny Murphy. "This is Mrs. Irelan at the depot," she said. "I need some help. There's a man over here demanding food, and he won't go away."

"We'll do something about that," the man who owned the store said.

My mother hung up, went back to the ticket window, and looked out at the tramp, who was still stomping around the waiting room. "He just went on and on," she recalled. "He ranted and raved. But in a minute or two I looked out the window and here came some of the men from the store. The tramp saw them coming and went straight out the door and took off down the track. I never saw him again."

"A week or two later," she said, "one of the section men found a mark some tramp had put on one of the tracks not far away. It was a signal to the other tramps that they could get a meal at the depot. The section man cleaned it off, and the tramps stopped coming through the door."

Like all the stories my mother told me when I was a child, she told this one over and over, so that I can type it now almost as if I were taking dictation. But it occurred to me only recently how remarkable it was that on that day in Murphy, Nebraska, when my mother needed help, she called a grocery store. And just as she knew it would, help arrived, and quickly. From a grocery store.

SALEM

By the spring of 1941, my father had accumulated enough seniority to bid successfully on jobs in Iowa, jobs that would bring his little family closer to its many relatives. In May of that year, he obtained the position of second-trick agent in the prosperous town of Mount Pleasant, Iowa, on the main line of the CB&Q. My sister remembers this period fondly. The family lived in a cheerful, spacious apartment on the second floor of a large house. But equally important to Jane, who was five years old, was the beautiful park across the street. That fall, she started to school, where, like her mother, she always excelled.

My father celebrated his thirty-fifth birthday on December 1, 1941. Six days later, the Empire of Japan spoiled the celebration by attacking American forces at Pearl Harbor and elsewhere in the Pacific. Pete had previously registered for the draft in Seward County, Nebraska, the county in which Milford is located. After the Japanese attack, he quickly informed the draft board in Seward County of his new address. Much less quickly, the overwhelmed Selective Service System informed my father that his railroad skills were essential to the success of the war effort and that the government regretted that it would not require his services in the armed forces.

The Selective Service System correctly understood the importance of railroads in warfare. From the American Civil War through World War II, weapons and troops moved increasingly by rail. Day after day in the early 1940s the trains rolled westward on the CB&Q, the freights loaded with weapons, the passenger trains filled with soldiers who would fight and die on Pacific islands they had never heard of.

Early in 1942, the family moved to the tiny village of Birmingham, where my mother had acquired the custodianship of the depot, and my father resumed his travels, now more important than ever, on the main line of the Burlington Railroad, which passed through the busy town of Fairfield only nine miles to the north.

According to his notebooks, Pete's assignments took him repeatedly during the next six years to Fairfield, Mount Pleasant, Ottumwa,

Lockridge, Batavia, New Virginia, the tower at the Lawler freight yard, Agency, Danville, Middletown, Beckwith, New London, West Burlington, Maxon, Chillicothe (Iowa), and the Ottumwa freight yard.

Early in the war, when my grandfather Irelan was seventy-three years old, he wrote a letter to my parents. Grandma Irelan had died eight years before I was born, and I remember seeing my grandpa only once in my life; but this four-page handwritten letter, which my sister and I recently discovered in my mother's effects, tells more about Grandpa Irelan than my parents or any other relative ever did. I will quote only a portion of the letter, which begins with the compulsive levity of the Irelan male, but ends with a different tone.

> Drakesville
> March 2, 1942
>
> Dear Kids,
>
> I thought I would write you a short note. I am getting along all right now. Had a little kick up early, but am about back to normal.
>
> How come you moved to Birmingham? I have been told that the R.R. runs up there and stops in a cow pasture and that the town has been dead for 20 years. I think I will come down this summer if the old car holds up and I can get gas. Want to go to Ottumwa one day this week if I can. John Haynes and Elmer Pierson both want to go.
>
> This town is getting to be a quiet place. All the men are gone. Merve McElderry has been called to the army and will go in a week or 10 days. Butch Schlarbaum will go too.
>
> I want to raise a garden this summer. I have to buy everything I eat now, and it costs to eat in this town. This war is not looking any too good now. It is going to cost many a poor boy's life, boys who don't know whose oil well or rubber plantation they are fighting for.
>
> It is about train time. Will write again later.
>
> Dad

Both Merve McElderry and Butch Schlarbaum survived the war. My grandfather, who had lost his farm during the Depression, died in destitution in 1950.

On February 2, 1943, in defiance of orders from Adolph Hitler, General Friedrich von Paulus surrendered the remnants of the German Sixth

Army to the Red Army at Stalingrad, an event that historians now recognize as the turning point of World War II in Europe.

Historians have also remained silent about another event that occurred in 1943. On March 25, shortly after the German surrender at
Stalingrad, Patrick Irelan entered the world via Caesarean section at
the Jefferson County Hospital in Fairfield, Iowa.

The entire hospital bill for this event totaled $115.00 — $37.50 more
than the bill from the Ottumwa Hospital for my sister's birth seven
years earlier. The statement includes sixteen days of care for mother
and child at $5.00 per day — $1.00 per day more than charged for my
mother and sister. By contrast, the Jefferson County Hospital charged
only $10.00 for use of the operating room — fifty cents less than the
amount charged by the Ottumwa Hospital.

The statement includes numerous smaller charges for other supplies
and services, most of which I cannot read because of the poor pen-
manship of the unknown person who wrote the bill, a person whose il-
legible signature appears at the bottom. In any event, my father paid
the bill in full the day that mother and child left the hospital.

By the time of my widely ignored birth, my parents and sister had
moved to Salem, Iowa, a village about twelve miles south of Mount
Pleasant. Here again the familiar pattern emerged. My mother served
as the custodian at Salem while my father went wherever the CB&Q
sent him on the main line.

While Mother was still in the hospital at Fairfield with little Patrick,
my father sent her a number of letters from Salem. He typed one of
these on the official letterhead of the Chicago, Burlington & Quincy
Railroad Company. This use of company property for private corre-
spondence seems entirely justifiable to me, given that the letter reveals
how my family's personal life had by then become inseparable from its
association with the railroad:

Salem, Apr. 5, 1943

Hello Sweetheart,

How are you getting along today? We are OK. Somewhat warmer
this PM and I am somewhat lazy. Nally called me this morning
and wanted me to go to Fairfield and leave Mrs. Irelan in charge at
Salem, so see what you missed by being in bed.

The 3rd trick Wood tower was on bulletin, so I suppose the
3rd trick man decided to take 2nd. Also put an operator [telegra-

pher] on at Clarkson 3 PM to 11 PM, and that was on bulletin. I didn't bid.

Grippen said that Bert Moore's sister would probably work for us, and that she is pretty good. I won't ask her until we find out for sure if Cora [a friend from Nebraska] is coming. Have my work pretty well caught up now. The depot could stand a little cleaning.

Jane and I will be over to see you Tuesday evening if the weather is nice and nothing interferes. Guess I can't think of anything to say right now, so will run up town and collect a few $ for the Quincy.

Love,

Daddy and Jane

I spent the first two years of my life in Salem and retain only one memory of that little village. The memory includes a tree-lined residential street. At the end of the street stands a small depot, and beyond the depot is a railroad track. Beyond the track, open fields reach into the distance. That's it. My earliest recollection in this life. I no doubt possess this recollection because my mother took me down that street with her every day when she walked to work at the depot.

My sister has far more vivid memories, including what seemed to her like endless clouds of airplanes, flying in formation all day long, day after day. What she cannot remember is the direction in which they were headed. This has led us to speculate that they were military airplanes en route from factories on the West Coast to bases on the East Coast, from where they would fly or be transported by ship to England. From there, they would join the Soviet Union, Britain, and our other allies in the long, deadly work of reducing German cities to the rubble, cinders, and ashes they would become by 1945.

But while Jane was watching the airplanes flying over Salem, my father was planning other conquests. He could not give up the idea of farming. But this time he would work for the railroad and run the farm simultaneously. One job is enough for most people, but my father had to have two. He would not be content until he had worked himself to death.

Thus it happened that on February 24, 1945, my parents purchased an eighty-acre farm two miles north of Bloomfield in Davis County for the sum of $3,200. The seller was a woman who inherited the farm at the age of eleven when her mother had died eighteen years before. Her uncle had always managed the farm for her. It was, in fact, the same farm on which my parents and sister had been living in 1937 when the CB&Q first hired my father.

Regrettably, this farm possessed almost no agricultural value, which explains how my parents could afford to buy it. But regardless of its value, it became in 1945 the place where my sister and I would spend the rest of our childhoods and where my father and mother would spend the rest of their lives. For all of us, the farm and the railroad became inseparable. I'm not sure it was a good union, but because I was only two, my vote didn't count.

THE FARM

One windy summer day during the drought of 1955, I was standing in the front yard of our farmhouse when I saw a huge red cloud approaching from the southwest. I had never seen anything like it before, and I ran inside to ask my mother what it was. She walked over to the kitchen window and said, "Oh my God, it's a dust storm. Help me close the doors and windows."

We closed everything as fast as we could and placed wet towels on the sills to keep the dust from blowing under the windows. Then we went back into the kitchen to watch the storm advance. Unlike normal clouds, which everyone hoped would bring rain from the heavens, this massive cloud traveled along the surface of the earth, gradually engulfing everything in its path.

In the town of Bloomfield two miles to the southwest, we could still see the clock tower of the Davis County Courthouse rising above the trees, but that soon faded behind the advancing cloud. Minutes later, the dust obscured Reno's sale barn at the south edge of town. Then the trees at the top of the hill north of the Fox River disappeared. The gravel road at the south end of our lane vanished next. Finally, the cloud consumed our little house, the yard, and the barn, leaving us alone in a dry red fog. I moved over and leaned against my mother. She put her arm around me. "Don't worry, Patrick," she said. "It will pass."

The next morning, the *Des Moines Register* reported that the dust storm had originated in Oklahoma, which accounted for its redness. But this did little to calm the anxiety of farmers in southern Iowa, who feared a return to the dry conditions of the 1930s. Among those who worried most were my parents, for time had not been kind to our small farm, and it would be a sure candidate for further devastation if the drought continued another year. Fortunately, it didn't continue.

The United States government had originally sold our farm in two forty-acre parcels in 1847. Subsequently, someone bought both of these parcels and combined them into the eighty-acre farm where I later grew up. The abstract of title for the period from 1847 to 1945, the year my parents bought the farm, contains thirty-one pages. These thirty-one pages tell a ninety-eight-year story of successes, failures, marriages, betrayals, divorces, deaths, lawsuits, foreclosures, and sheriff's sales.

By 1945, the land itself told a story of the previous ninety-eight years, and this story paid few compliments to the previous owners and tenants. In a fashion that was far too common, many of the pioneers had plowed hillsides that should never have been plowed and planted crops year after year that depleted the soil of nitrogen and other nutrients. In the mentality of these pioneers, there was, after all, always another inexpensive farm farther west. By 1945, the soil on our farm had lost its fertility and gullies scarred the hillsides, and there were no more inexpensive farms farther west.

My father immediately began a program of remedial farming. On the hilly land, he sowed lespedeza and alfalfa, legumes that would restore nitrogen to that land, which he would use only for pasture. To these legumes, he added the Kentucky bluegrass that cattle crave. On the farm's one flat field, he sowed a mixture of timothy and clover to use as hay for the Angus calves and two milk cows he would soon buy. Invariably, scattered shoots of Queen Anne's lace grew up here and there amidst the timothy and clover, turning the meadow into one of those lovely miracles that nature sometimes grants us. For many years, my father planted no corn at all, corn being the crop that most injures soil fertility. Instead, he bought whatever corn he needed for his calves. And on every spot of ground he could reach, he spread manure that would, along with these other measures, restore the soil's health.

According to the theory of that era, this program would ultimately heal the gullies on the hillsides, and on most of the farm this theory proved successful. But on one hillside, where the gullies reached four feet deep, my father finally hired a man with a bulldozer to help the theory along.

Eventually, the farm began to look more like what nature had intended, but the price my father paid for that success was a life of endless toil. After we moved to the farm, my mother gave up railroad work and returned to schoolteaching, but my father continued to work as a depot agent. Five days a week he went to work on the railroad, and every minute he spent at home during daylight hours, he worked on the farm. He wouldn't sleep until it became too dark to work. He slept soundly, but never for very long.

I cannot forget the hundreds of nights my mother woke him from a sound sleep. "Daddy Pete," she would say, placing her hand on his arm, "it's time to wake up." He always had a depot waiting for him somewhere, and he had to be there on time. He worked in an industry in which disasters occurred unless all the workers did their jobs, and he couldn't ask someone else to stay an extra eight hours to cover for him just because he was tired. I am convinced that too much work and too little sleep shortened his life, and I don't believe those eighty acres were worth it.

―――――――

As a little boy, the only farm work I could do was pump water for the cattle, which I normally did in the company of my sister. At the bottom of a hill toward the back of the farm, some pioneer had dug a shallow well and installed a pump. Every summer, Jane and I walked back to this pump twice each day and began the negotiations to determine how much work each of us would do. Because she was older and stronger than I, we agreed from the outset that she would pump more than I. The only issue was how much more. "I'll pump a hundred strokes for every seventy-five you pump," she would say.

"Seventy-five?" I said, feigning exhaustion at the mere thought of it. "How about twenty-five?"

"How about fifty?" she said as the jury of cattle stared at us with their huge brown eyes.

"All right," I said, knowing from past experience that this was the best deal I would get.

Jane would begin pumping as the larger cattle butted the smaller ones aside to get at the water that came gushing down the trough from the pump to the tank. After her first hundred strokes, I began the slow process of lifting the handle and pushing it down. At about thirty-five strokes, I stopped working and fell back against the wooden fence that surrounded the pump. "That wasn't fifty," Jane said.

"Yes it was," I lied.

"It wasn't even forty."

"It was fifty."

"Pump fifteen more."

The cattle had started bellowing by this point. I pumped another fifteen. "There," I said. "Now it's your turn."

The argument went on and on. Although I hate to confess to such wickedness, I don't think I ever pumped all fifty strokes without being forced to. While the struggle continued between Jane and me, the struggle continued among the cattle. I never pumped my fifty strokes without a series of charges and denials. The smaller cattle never reached the tank until the larger ones had drunk their fill.

Our instructions required us to pump until the last calf had quenched its thirst and then leave the tank full when we finally walked away. Unless you have lived on a cattle farm, you would be amazed at how much water twenty Angus steers can drink. As far as I know, none of the cattle ever died of thirst, although I frequently claimed that I would drop dead if I had to pump another stroke.

After the wells went dry during the drought of 1955, my father began a program of pond building, as did a great many other cattle farmers in southern Iowa. Bulldozers arrived and began gnawing at the hillsides, throwing up earthen dams that would collect the runoff from the rains that finally returned. Over the years, as he could afford it, Pete built three ponds in all. The pump at the back of the farm fell into disuse. The calves no longer gathered to push and bellow. The debates over the difference between thirty-five and fifty strokes fell silent.

———

By the time I reached thirteen, I had acquired the strength to help my father with heavier farm work. "Patrick," he would say as we set out on some project, "if you do a job right the first time, you won't have to do it again." I always saw the intelligence of this advice, although I found it difficult to follow. I lacked his manual dexterity and eye-hand coordination, and felt myself lucky if I could complete a job at all.

"Never use a machine to do something you can do by hand," was another of his maxims. In putting this notion into practice, I found that it all too often applied to *my* hands. When we built a fence, he would mark the spot where each post should go in order to make the fence perfectly straight. Then I dug the holes by hand. All of them. My father then put the posts into the holes and held them admirably straight while I shoveled the dirt back in and tamped it down. "Do the job right and you'll have something worth keeping," he said by way of encouragement as I shoveled and tamped.

When the soil on our farm had finally been restored to something approximating its original fertility, we would plant a few acres

[T H E   F A R M]

of corn every year, but never two years in a row in the same place. Using our little Ford tractor, I learned how to plow a reasonably straight furrow, although my father didn't hesitate to point out the numerous imperfections in my work. Disking and harrowing the soil were so easy that even I could manage those tasks without the need of lengthy critiques.

Rather than buying a new or used corn planter for the tractor, my father adapted an old two-row planter built originally for horses. In tasks such as these, his true genius shone through. Other farmers would stare in amazement at this corn planter, no doubt thinking of all the money they had spent on new machines.

I don't know if I could plant a straight row of corn or not. My father wisely never let me try. If the rows weren't straight, you couldn't cultivate them properly and the weeds would overwhelm the corn. Pete did, however, let me help him pick the corn, which we did by hand. I believe we were the last farmers in North America who picked our corn by hand, although there may have been one or two others in some remote part of Manitoba reachable only by helicopter.

For every ear of corn that I picked, Pete would pick four or five. He never criticized me for my slowness. He knew that some children were gifted and others were not. The important thing was to pick every ear and leave none behind. Only a human being can do this. No corn picker ever built can pick every ear, and my father hated waste. Poverty can do that to a man. A summer with nothing to eat but milk and eggplant can do it.

By the age of fourteen, I had acquired the strength for heavy work. I don't know what farm boys are like nowadays, but when I was a boy, we reveled in heat and hard work. Two of us would stand in the haymow and stack sixty-pound hay bales as high as we could reach, then go to the door and shout "More hay!" to the boy on the wagon who was trying to put the bales on the elevator fast enough to overwhelm us. While this contest proceeded, two more boys were stacking bales six high on another hay wagon out in the field as the baler spat them out.

At the end of the day, when all the hay was in the mow, protracted negotiations would begin between my father and Ira Raisch, the only man in the neighborhood who owned a hay baler. Ira was trim and muscular. He had dark hair, a permanently tanned face, and the whitest teeth I've ever seen.

"How much do I owe you?" Pete would say.

"You don't owe me anything. All I did was drive the tractor," Ira said, referring to the tractor that pulled the baler.

"Ira, you can't work for nothing. That's an expensive machine you have there. You'll wear it out working for the neighbors, and you have to buy gas for the tractor."

"Okay, a penny a bale," Ira said.

"A penny a bale? That won't even buy you a pot to pee in. I won't take advantage of a man like that."

"All right, two cents."

"Two cents?" Pete said. "Ira, I don't have much money, but I can afford to pay what the job's worth."

This would go on for some time. All the boys were tired, so no one minded sitting on the well curb, drinking what seemed like the coldest water in the state. I don't recall what price Pete and Ira would finally arrive at, but it was always less than what the job was worth. By long-standing tradition, the farmers paid the boys a dollar an hour for putting up hay, and I worked for all the farmers who asked me. That dollar an hour is the only honest money I've ever earned.

Pete finally began to make a modest profit as a cattle farmer. He bought young calves and fed them for the two years it took them to grow to market weight. Then he sold them at auction at Reno's sale barn in Bloomfield or directly to Morrell's packinghouse in Ottumwa. Sometimes he sold his steers to professional cattle traders, men referred to by the cattle farmers in our neighborhood as "scalpers."

Each method of selling your calves had its advantages and disadvantages. If sold at auction, the steers went to the bidder who offered the most per pound. Then the sale barn immediately weighed the calves and there was no cause for disagreement. The disadvantages were that you might not get the price you wanted and that the sale barn kept a small percentage of the sale price for its services.

If you took the steers directly to the packinghouse, you knew in advance, by looking in a newspaper or listening to the radio, about how much the packing plants were paying for cattle that week. The company's buyer would offer you a price per pound based on his estimate of the quality of the meat the steer would produce. At that time, the best meat would go to expensive restaurants on the East Coast. The average meat would go to restaurants and grocery stores in the Middle

West. The worst went into various canned products I dare not name for fear of libel suits. After the buyer made his offer, you argued awhile. Then it became a matter of take it or leave it. If you took it, they weighed the calves and you went home with a check. If you declined the offer, you still owned the calves, but you had to pay the trucker to haul them back home. Then you had to keep feeding them. Most farmers took the check.

Dealing with a scalper resembled an aggressive form of gambling. First you argued with him about the price per pound. Then you argued with him about the weight of each calf. To come out ahead, the farmer had to be able to estimate the calf's weight accurately. If you thought the calf weighed less than it actually did, you would lose money. But if the scalper thought it weighed more than it actually did, you would make money. If you accepted the scalper's offer, he wrote you a check and a truck soon appeared to haul the steers away.

Regardless of how he sold his steers, my father always walked into the house afterward and said, "Mother, we took a terrible beating on the calves." Then he would spell it out in great detail, and gradually you began to see that he hadn't taken the terrible beating he claimed. He just hadn't made as much as he wanted, and he considered that a failure.

My father took me with him to observe all these aspects of the cattle business. We went to the sale barn every Saturday, regardless of whether Pete intended to buy or sell a thing. The sale barn included the pens in back where the livestock stood around waiting to be sold. The auction area itself formed a semicircle similar to an ancient Greek theater, but with a roof. The livestock ring stood at the bottom, where the stage would be in the theater.

From the viewpoint of the people in the crowd, the livestock entered the ring through a gate on the right and went out through a gate on the left. On an elevated platform at the back of the ring, the auctioneer, who always wore a straw cowboy hat, sat behind a microphone at a long, narrow desk. One or more clerks sat beside him to record each sale. All the auctioneers were men. Some of the clerks were men. Some were women. When the auctioneer's voice grew tired, another man in a straw cowboy hat replaced him. They continued to take turns throughout the sale, which would start early in the morning and last until late in the afternoon.

I don't know why the auctioneers wore straw cowboy hats. The hats looked good until you walked outside, when the wind immediately blew them away. That's why all the other men and boys wore caps. They kept the sun out of your eyes and stayed on your head. Seed-corn and farm-equipment companies now give caps to farmers. A woman from Chicago once asked me how she could get a seed-corn cap. I told her to buy two thousand dollars worth of seed corn and they would give her all the caps she wanted.

At each sale, the sheep, hogs, and cattle all sold at different times of the day, so you didn't have to look at a lot of sheep when you were interested only in cattle. If you arrived early and grew faint from hunger while waiting for the beef cattle to appear, you could always go down to the little café beneath the semicircle of seats for a hamburger or a piece of pie and a cup of coffee. The café sold excellent food and coffee, although I did hear farmwives comment occasionally on the relative lack of cleanliness in the place, which was located, after all, in a barn.

Gradually, as I attended sale after sale, I learned to understand what the auctioneer was saying. Auctioneers don't talk fast because they're in a hurry to go home and watch roller derby on TV. They're trying instead to get the buyers into a rhythm that allows little time for reflection or second thoughts. They want them to bid and keep on bidding. This theory underlies the auctioneer's method, but I doubt that it actually works that way. At every sale I attended, when a steer entered the auction ring, every farmer or packinghouse buyer in the barn instantly knew how much he was prepared to bid, and a fast-talking auctioneer wouldn't change his mind. The most skillful buyers had already looked at the cattle in the holding pens before the sale ever started. It did bring pleasure, though, to listen to a good auctioneer. The best recalled the pitch and rhythm of Appalachian speech, and the auctioneers at Reno's were among the best. Nothing could deny you the music of their voices.

As I grew more familiar with the protocol of the sale barn, I saw how each man would bid in some subtle manner, such as a slight nod of the head or the movement of a finger. Two tall, lean men in blue overalls always stood down in the ring to keep the livestock moving so that everyone got a good look. The men in the ring also helped the auctioneer by watching for bids, which they then acknowledged with a loud "Yeah."

At least once during each auction, someone would become confused about who had bid what and when for the cattle in the ring. This always occasioned much joking among the other farmers about people bidding against themselves or against their spouses. While this entertainment continued, the auctioneer and clerks conferred about the series of bids. No one ever expressed anger about these events. Everyone in the sale barn knew everyone else, and no one would ever have said a word to offend anyone. Finally, after more jokes from the comedians in the crowd, the auctioneer would summarize the previous bids to everyone's satisfaction, and the sale would continue until the last calf, sheep, or hog had found a new owner.

Over the years, I learned how to judge the quality of a calf by the straightness of its back, the firmness of its belly, the broadness of its haunches, the health of its eyes, and other qualities. Finally, I learned how to guess a steer's weight, which is something you can learn only from years of observation and experience. It's one of those skills that no one can teach you, not even your father.

I never felt more surprised than the day my father first asked me to guess the weight of a steer. I must have been sixteen by then. I had always assumed that Pete wouldn't ask my opinion about anything that important until an angel appeared on the barn roof. I leaned against the top board of the barnyard fence and took my time looking at the calf, just the way Pete would have done it. Then I said, "Nine seventy-five."

"I think you're a little high," he said. "I'd guess nine fifty."

That was the best calf he owned that year. He sold it by itself the next day at Reno's sale barn, then sold five or six others in one lot. That one steer weighed nine hundred and eighty pounds.

"Good guess," Pete said after picking up his check from the woman at the cashier's window, a check that returned a good profit on those steers.

"Thanks," I said, taking care to repress any display of vanity.

After the sale, we drove home and walked into the house, where Pete sat down at the kitchen table and said, "Mother, we took a terrible beating on the calves."

Every schoolteacher knows that children learn more as class size decreases. For this reason, the best education occurs in classes with one teacher and one student. Quite by chance, this precise ratio existed during my entire nine years in grade school, for I attended a one-room country school and was the only student in my grade during each of those nine years. This does not mean that I was a brilliant student. But I did the best I could, given my brain capacity, hereditary gifts, and appropriate eyeglasses. For one-ninth of every school day, the teacher's attention focused entirely on me, and neither the teacher nor I squandered that time. For the rest of the day, I prepared my lessons and read the books of Mark Twain that stood in our school library, a library consisting of six-foot-wide, glass-enclosed shelves that reached from floor to ceiling. This library contained five of Twain's books. When I finished reading them, I started over and read them again. I did this year after year. I read other books as well, but I liked Twain better than any other writer and still do.

If my eyes grew weary on an autumn day, I would gaze out the windows along the east wall at the industrious red squirrels in the black walnut trees. In the winter I would gaze at the snow-covered fields. In the spring the red squirrels came out again. The town in which I presently live, which lies about sixty miles north and forty miles east of where I went to grade school, contains only gray squirrels. I read in a local newspaper that the aggressive red squirrels are driving the gray squirrels northward. I subsequently read in the same newspaper that the aggressive gray squirrels are driving the red squirrels southward. The squirrels apparently read no newspapers at all, for during my frequent drives between these two locations I have seen no change in where the red and gray squirrels live.

If I felt the need for visual stimulation inside the schoolroom, I looked at the black-and-white reproduction of a portrait of George Washington hanging on the north wall, or at the last photograph ever taken of Abraham Lincoln, the one with the crack in the negative, that hung on the south wall. The teachers at my school taught us to revere Abraham Lincoln. I absorbed that lesson and have never questioned it. When I grew old enough to drive a car, I drove my mother and my aunt Thelma, both of whom were schoolteachers, to Springfield, Illinois, where we toured Lincoln's home, drove across town, and walked in absolute silence through the tomb of Mrs. Lincoln and our martyred president. I have never taken a better trip than that one.

Because each student had plenty of time to complete his or her assignments during the day, the teachers never uttered the word "homework." When farm children, especially the older ones, arrived home after school, they had farm work to do. The teachers all knew this and acted accordingly. At harvest time the older boys often became sick — so sick that they had to spend entire days picking corn. This proved to be the perfect treatment for their symptoms, and once they had shoveled the last ears of corn into the cribs, the boys immediately recovered and returned to school, where the teacher greeted them as if they had never been absent.

When not preparing my lessons, reading Mark Twain, or looking at the fields, trees, and squirrels through the windows, I would listen as the older students recited their lessons. This suggests another well-known advantage of the one-room country school: The younger children continually heard the older students telling the teacher what they had learned. By listening to the recitations of the older students, the younger students couldn't help but learn in advance the material they would study in subsequent years. By the time I entered the eighth grade, I already knew everything the teacher intended to teach me. This did not result from any inborn genius. It resulted, instead, from something else that every schoolteacher knows: Repeat the lesson often enough by whatever means you have, and the child will learn it. Perhaps I should digress at this point and explain that I eventually taught school for five years and never met another teacher who challenged these bold claims I've made about what "every schoolteacher knows." In fact, it was the older, more experienced teachers who first voiced these claims to me.

I have already alluded to the educational setting provided for me and my fellow scholars: a solid wall of windows on the east, Washington on the north, Lincoln on the south, and a row of slate blackboards on the west, before which the teacher sat in a wooden swivel chair at a large oak desk and saw to the preparation of our young minds. The room came well equipped with pull-down maps of every place on earth, a large globe, and desks of every size for every child. All the modern amenities advanced the educational process: a large coal stove, electric lights, a pump only a few yards from the front door, a coal shed, and two gender-specific outhouses.

The schoolyard provided every advantage needed for the physical well-being of the children. First of all, it was very large, allowing enough room for any childhood game we could imagine. All the boy's games involved running. We ran for fifteen minutes during morning recess and for another fifteen minutes during afternoon recess. At noon we grabbed our dinner buckets, speedily devoured the food our mothers had prepared, and ran for the remaining portion of the sixty-minute dinner hour.

Our equipment included a ball, a bat, a basketball, a basketball hoop, a football, a large maple tree that we were forbidden to climb, but which we climbed anyway, and a deep grader ditch between the schoolyard and the road, where we played endless games of cops and robbers that resulted in thousands of deaths by gunfire, all of which caused the victims to fall into the ditch and roll all the way to the bottom. At times we could induce the girls to join us at softball in order to have enough players for both the infield and outfield. But for the most part, the girls met in small groups and engaged in secretive conversations, the contents of which they never revealed to mere boys.

In all honesty, I must now acknowledge that one-room country schools did have two disadvantages. The first of these involved the hiring of teachers. The school board, which consisted of officers elected by the voters living in the area the school served, had the responsibility of hiring or rehiring the teacher each year, making use of the personnel files that the county superintendent of schools maintained. If the school board hired a bad teacher, it hired that teacher for all the children in all the grades. That teacher could waste an entire year for every child in the school.

The school board had the option of firing the teacher, but that could lead to costly lawsuits, and school boards made up of farmers generally avoided anything costly. The usual practice was to wait until the end of the year and not invite the bonehead back for a second try. Then, by word of mouth, the members of the school board told every other school board in the county about their dissatisfaction with that teacher, who either found a new profession or moved away to work his or her damage elsewhere. Most of my teachers were excellent, two were average, and one was a bonehead. Quite by coincidence, the board had hired this one bad teacher for my first year in school. Her main shortcoming lay in the fact that she didn't understand children, which, in a schoolteacher, is comparable to an auto mechanic who doesn't understand internal-combustion engines.

Two years before my first year in school, at the age of three, I had run across East Williams Street in Ottumwa one night into the path of an oncoming gravel truck. Luckily, the driver was already slowing down for the stop sign at South Sheridan Avenue, and he possessed both quick reflexes and great presence of mind. After instantly stopping the truck, he set the brakes, jumped from the cab with his flashlight already turned on, and ran to the front. There he saw that I was fully conscious, that the left front wheel was resting on my left leg, and that if he had not stopped when he did, the wheel would have passed across my stomach. He climbed back into the cab, put the transmission into reverse, and slowly backed the truck off my broken leg.

During the next six months, Dr. Moore, a local surgeon, first set the bone, then operated on my leg twice when the break didn't heal properly. I spent most of those six months in St. Joseph's Hospital in Ottumwa. I remember nothing of this period except starting across the street, going home six months later, and the smell of ether, sensations of which occasionally surface in my mind when I am in places such as parks, libraries, farm fields, or other locations where no one would ever encounter the smell of ether. Although I remember neither the accident nor the hospital, I'm sure all these events happened, because my mother said they did and because I have a nine-inch scar on my left thigh.

As a consequence of this accident, when I started to school at the age of five, my leg still pained me all too frequently. The pain made me fidgety and restless as I sat at my desk, and this behavior annoyed the teacher, who thought it could be cured by having me stand in the corner. As anyone with the brains of a red squirrel could predict, this merely exacerbated the problem by causing more pain, more restlessness, and more time in the corner. My sister, who attended the same school, reported these events to my parents, who had already noticed an unhappiness in their normally happy little boy.

My mother took me to see Dr. Fenton, our family physician, one of the last of the old-fashioned country doctors. He unlocked his office above Augspurger's Hardware Store on the west side of the town square in Bloomfield early every morning, saw the patients in the order in which they arrived, and stayed until he had treated everyone, even if it took until midnight, as it sometimes did.

You reached Dr. Fenton's office by climbing an open flight of stairs on the exterior wall at the south end of the block. The waiting room was roughly square in shape, with chairs placed closely together along three walls. Most of the men who sat in these chairs wore overalls, and most of the women wore simple cotton dresses. In the summer, a hassock fan stood in the center of the room, although I don't know if it made anyone feel cooler. A desk for the woman who acted as the receptionist and bookkeeper stood near the back wall. The back wall also had a door leading to a maze of offices, examining rooms, and storage rooms, all of which was so complex that little boys dared not let go of their mothers' hands for fear of getting lost forever.

Dr. Fenton left the office only to see patients at the hospital, to perform surgery, to make house calls for the very ill, or to carry out his duties as the county coroner. His bookkeeper kept records but never sent out bills. People paid him if and when they had the money. Some of the poorest people would never have the money. Dr. Fenton knew this, and he didn't care.

By the time of my earliest memory of him, Dr. Fenton had gray hair, which he wore closely cropped so that it would never obscure his vision or require the use of a comb when more important matters needed his attention. I recall that he was above average in height and had blue eyes, but I couldn't promise either of these for sure. I can say with greater certainty that he had an intelligent face, regular features, and a placid bearing. I have never seen or met a more imperturbable man or woman in my life. He never hurried and never stopped working, thereby treating more patients on a typical day than any other doctor in town. The kind, consistent, never-ceasing manner of his work caused his patients to regard him with absolute faith.

Nothing ever disturbed or excited Dr. Fenton in any way that would interfere with the important tasks he performed. One day he walked into his waiting room and said, "A man over by Floris just killed his wife and committed suicide, so I'll be gone for an hour or two." Then he walked out the door and down the stairs. No one complained. Everybody knew that he was the coroner and that he would come back as soon as he could. One of my mother's friends, who was sitting in the waiting room that day, reported that he made this announcement with no more emotion than he might have shown if he were going out for a sandwich. He combined in one personality the qualities of compassion and calmness, which explained why people waited hours for him if necessary. He would take their problems seriously, but without alarm, calm their worst fears, give them all the time and attention they needed, and take care of them no matter what.

On the day Mother took me to Dr. Fenton's office, we waited about an hour before a nurse showed us into an examining room. Dr. Fenton came in ten minutes later, and my mother told him why we had come. He examined my leg, watched me walk back and forth, and watched me jump up and down. He held me on his lap, asked me where I got those blue eyes, and told me I looked a lot like my daddy. Then he talked to me for a long time, asked me many questions, saw my unhappiness, and said to my mother, "Gerata, unless this teacher changes her ways, we'll have to take the boy out of school. She's doing him harm that could be more damaging in the long run than a broken bone." He paused when he saw the tears in my mother's eyes. "We don't need to get too upset about this," he said gently, "but we do need to do something about it." He paused again while Mother wiped her eyes. "Where's Pete working today?" he asked.

"The Eldon yard."

"Good. So he'll be home tonight?"

"Yes."

"That's soon enough. You and Pete can talk about this tonight and decide what to do. I think going straight to the superintendent's office wouldn't be a bad idea. I'll go with you if you want me to. Mr. Milligan and I have never disagreed about anything, and we're not likely to start now." Both my mother and father had become friends of Dr. Fenton's at Bloomfield High School twenty-five years before, he knew every important thing there was to know about our family, and my parents understood that they could rely on his judgment and advice. If he told them something needed to be done, they would do it. Dr. Fenton lifted me from his lap, stood me on the floor, and said, "Patrick, tell your daddy I said not to get those boxcars all mixed up."

My mother drove us home and kept me out of school the rest of the day. She wanted to call my father right then, but he was working in the tower at the freight yard in Eldon, and distracting him at the wrong moment could result in sending a load of steel back to Gary, Indiana, when someone still wanted it in Kansas City. So she called my aunt, Blanch

Irelan Wells, instead. We should not mistake this aunt Blanch for my other aunt Blanche, who had married Uncle Cliff Irelan and lived in Newton. I also had two Uncle Cliffs. Confusions of this sort arise in large families.

Aunt Blanch Wells lived with Uncle Joe and my cousin Dean on a farm less than a mile down the road from our house and farm. My cousin Helen had already married by this date and lived with her family on another farm. Aunt Blanch had been born in 1890, the first of my father's eleven brothers and sisters, all of whom grew up on a farm near Drakesville, except for little Clayton, who died of an accident at age two. I don't claim to know how the human personality develops, but I suspect that being the oldest of twelve children might have given Aunt Blanch more self-confidence and assertiveness than she would have possessed if she had been born last. I should also point out that Aunt Blanch, like all my aunts and one of my uncles, had been a school-teacher herself, and by all accounts a good one. To all these qualities, add these: Her white hair implied the authority and wisdom that come with age, she possessed an imposing presence, and she had more intelligence than the entire United States Senate. When my mother called, Aunt Blanch grasped the nature of the problem instantly and expressed her sympathy in the strongest terms. She did not, however, tell my mother what to do or how to do it.

Nonetheless, when Jane left school that afternoon, she couldn't help noticing that Aunt Blanch was sitting in her car, which was parked in the school driveway. Jane ran over and said, "Hello, Aunt Blanch. What are you doing here?"

"Oh, I just thought I'd visit the school and talk to the teacher awhile," Aunt Blanch said. "I used to be a teacher myself, you know."

"Yes, I know. Daddy says you were a good one."

"I did my best," Aunt Blanch said with a smile.

The other children who lived down the road in the direction of our house were waiting for Jane. She said good-bye and ran to catch up with the others, turning around once to wave at Aunt Blanch, who had already climbed out of her car. Aunt Blanch waved back, then started toward the school.

I don't know what Aunt Blanch said to the teacher that day. She never told my mother or father, and they were too polite to ask. To the best of my knowledge, the teacher never mentioned the conversation to anybody connected with the school. Given that Aunt Blanch's remarks could not have been flattering, the teacher probably never re-peated them to anyone. But whatever Aunt Blanch said had a profound and immediate effect on the behavior of that teacher. From that day on, she treated me with what appeared to be the greatest kindness.

Her kindness was insincere, of course. Children can sense insincer-ity in an adult every time. Nature equips children with that instinct as a means of self-defense. But I didn't care about her sincerity. I cared about her actions, as did Aunt Blanch, Dr. Fenton, and my parents. I was lucky that I had such an aunt, someone who knew what to do and wasn't afraid to do it. And as you have probably guessed, that teacher wasn't invited back the next year. The school board delivered us, in-stead, into the loving hands of Eva McMillin, the best schoolteacher this boy ever had. Unlike her predecessor, she understood everything about children.

———

The second potential disadvantage of a one-room country school was far less serious than the first, although it didn't necessarily seem less serious to a child. The second disadvantage was that one's mother or father might be hired as the teacher. This presented a nightmare of Kafkaesque dimensions. When I was nine years old, the Selective Ser-vice System, in its infinite cruelty, drafted the teacher of my school and shipped him off to the Korean War, where he suffered far less than I, for the entire school board suddenly fell victim to demonic possession and hired my mother to replace the young teacher until the war ended and he could return to the safety of southern Iowa.

Some readers may wonder if my mother gave me preferential treat-ment while serving as my teacher. Fear not. Quite the opposite was true. As far as my studies were concerned, I continued to do as well or ill as I had with my other teachers. My mother was an outstanding teacher. She instinctively knew how to draw the best performance pos-sible from each child, and she did not expect every child to perform the same. Each was an individual encouraged to compete only with him-self or herself. Early in her career, she received an endorsement from Mr. H. C. Brown, the county superintendent of schools, an endorse-ment so complimentary that it has to have been truthfully written:

> Miss Hunter is a "natural" teacher in every sense implied by the
> term. She controls and directs with a minimum of friction in the

school and in the community. She inherently loves children, and they, in turn, love her. Her teaching is lucid, vigorous, and sane. Her personality is pleasing and she makes and keeps friends wherever she is known.

The problem I encountered when my mother took charge of our little white schoolhouse lay in the field of deportment. From the other children, she expected normal behavior. From me, she expected Christ-like behavior. I couldn't possibly meet such expectations. Jesus and I didn't have the same father.

One spring day, a little boy came down with the flu, and my mother had to drive him home. She couldn't call the child's parents because the school didn't have a telephone. Before she left she said, "While I'm gone, I want all of you to continue with your studies. There is to be no talking." Then she turned to one of the youngest students, a little girl named Sally, and said, "When I get back, I will ask you to tell me if everyone followed my instructions." With that said, she left with the sick child.

After she had gone, only a few of the older children continued to study, but no one said anything. Most looked around at everyone else, waiting for something to happen. The situation presented a rare op-portunity for mischief, and few wanted to miss it when it occurred. For some reason known only to our Heavenly Father, the Devil chose exactly that moment to lead me into the wilderness for forty days and forty nights, where he sorely tempted me with every form of evil known to suffering humanity. I tried to withstand the tempter, but the beast within me began to stir. I suddenly realized that everyone in the room was looking at me. Or maybe the Devil only made it seem that everyone was looking at me. The evil one assailed me from all sides. I grew weak, then weaker, then weaker still. The beast rose within me like a Holly-wood reptile, and all my strength and all my resolve slipped away. I opened my mouth. I engaged my tongue and vocal cords. Air escaped from my lungs. "Well?" I said.

Bedlam erupted. Everyone seemed to talk at once, and in all truth-fulness, I must tell you that the most talkative of the talkers consisted of three or four girls of about my own age. As everyone knows, boys and girls emerge from the womb with a congenital hatred of each other. At about the age of thirteen or fourteen, hormonal events occur that cure this condition. Much later, domestic events sometimes restore this congenital hatred, but that problem does not belong in a discussion of my little white schoolhouse.

Back in the classroom, the remarks issuing from the small but relentless female contingent returned again and again to one theme. To little Sally, who seemed quite embarrassed and not flattered in the least by their attention, they repeatedly said, "Tell Mrs. Irelan Pat talked." Then they elaborated helpfully on the many ways in which Sally could emphasize the most heinous aspects of my crime. The boys addressed a few pointed insults at these girls and refused to join the conspiracy. But for the most part, they sat in silence, no doubt wondering why I had suddenly become completely brainless.

Finally, the oldest child in the school, an eighth-grade girl, shouted, "Shut up, all of you! I'm trying to read." Everyone shut up. I wonder where that girl is today. She's probably the CEO of a fifty-billion-dollar corporation somewhere. She showed definite leadership qualities that afternoon, but even she couldn't save me from the grim hand of justice.

Soon, much sooner than I would have liked, my mother's car pulled into the driveway. She walked inside and hung up her coat. By this point I was hoping for a miracle. Maybe Sally would fall into a coma that would last until our teacher returned from Korea. I knew that sudden comas were rare among five-year-old children, but I always try to remain hopeful in difficult situations.

Mother stood there, looking approvingly around the roomful of studious children. I was working furiously on an arithmetic problem. Maybe she'll forget, I hoped. She didn't forget. She smiled at Sally and said, "Sally, did everyone follow my instructions?" Everyone stared at Sally. Sally still didn't care for their attention. Her head drooped and she looked shyly from side to side. The perpetuation of ancient boy-girl hatreds hung in the balance. "Sally," my mother said again, gently, "did everyone follow my instructions?"

Sally stared at her desktop. "No," she said. Sighs of joy rose from the enemy camp. A boy looked at me the way you would look at a flat tire.

"Who didn't?" my mother said, with genuine surprise on her face.

Sally stared at her desk as if she were paralyzed. There was still time for a coma. "Pat," she said.

Silence, dead silence, silence like that which must exist inside a granite mountain. My mother's face suggested that a trusted friend had just stolen her best silverware, that the minister of her church had just uttered a series of blasphemies during his Sunday morning sermon, or that my grandmother had suddenly started drinking a fifth of gin every day.

Mother looked at the clock on the wall. "It's time for recess," she said. It wasn't really time for recess. Recess had been called into special session. Perhaps the governor would speak. "Pat," she said, "you stay inside. Everyone else is excused." The place emptied out like a speak-easy during a raid.

My mother sat down at her desk and looked silently at me. I considered suicide but lacked the necessary hardware. "Pat," she said. My mother always called me "Pat" when she was displeased with me. At all other times, she called me "Patrick." My father followed the same practice, which always provided me with a parental early-warning system. Unfortunately, the system did not include parent-proof shelters. "Pat," she said, "I had hoped that you of all people would not disobey my instructions." I didn't reply. "Why did you do it?"

"I don't know."

"You don't know?"

"Everyone was looking at me."

"Why were they looking at you?"

"I don't know."

"What did you say?"

"I said, 'Well?'"

"Well?"

"Yes."

"Why?"

"Because everyone was looking at me."

This admission elicited a long silence from my mother. I never lied to her, and she knew it. She was trying to make sense out of something senseless, and this always taxes the powers of the human mind. The human mind craves logic and order. This is what distinguishes it from a potato. "What else did you say?" she asked, probing for a spark of logic.

"Nothing." The spark failed to appear.

"What happened after you said it?"

"A bunch of girls began telling Sally what to tell you."

My mother took a deep breath and sat back in the chair. She saw the spark, and the spark ignited a bonfire. "So these girls started talking?"

"Yes."

"Who were they?"

I didn't answer. My mother allowed herself a slight smile. She had been a teacher for many years. She knew that little boys at that time and place did not tell on other children, even if the other children were their worst enemies. "Patrick," she said, "I've made a mistake. I was worried about Danny, and I asked a little girl to do something too complicated for her to do. I won't make that mistake again. If anything like this ever happens to you again, don't let anyone trick you into doing something you'll regret. I'll speak to Sally to make sure she isn't upset. We won't need to talk about this anymore. Recess will soon be over. You'd better get a drink and go to the toilet."

I stood up to go outside. "I'm sorry, Mother," I said.

I know that grade-school teachers sometimes hug their youngest students to comfort and encourage them, but my mother didn't hug me that day in our little school. She did what she always did. She waited until we got home.

BE FRUITFUL

One Sunday when I was in college, I drove over to Aunt Blanche and Uncle Cliff's house in Newton, Iowa, to meet with a small segment of the huge Irelan clan. We were drinking coffee and inhaling the odors from the kitchen when one of Uncle Cliff and Aunt Blanche's grandchildren, little Jennifer, walked into the room and said, "There's a man at the door who says he's working his way through college selling magazine subscriptions."

My cousin Norma, Jennifer's mother, immediately said, "Uncle Pete," and headed for the door while the rest of us followed. There on the steps stood my father, neatly dressed in a gray suit, looking as serious as a seventeenth-century Calvinist, while my mother stood tolerantly beside him. The significance of this event resided in the fact that my father always introduced himself this way when given the opportunity. For the rest of the day, he and my uncle Cliff entertained us with familiar stories from an imaginary past.

At dinner, my father reminded us that as children, he and each of his eleven brothers and sisters had been required to line up at the garden gate, wait for the dinner bell, and then race to the house and into the dining room before the others had devoured all the food. "Because I was one of the youngest and smallest," he said, "I was always one of the last." He then cited his childhood hunger as the cause of numerous alleged maladies, none of which has ever been listed or described in a medical textbook.

Uncle Cliff was taller and slightly older than my father, with a larger frame and eyes of a paler blue, but in every important respect — moral, intellectual, and social — they were identical. As was his custom, Uncle Cliff told everyone not to eat too much because, in spite of constant searching, he hadn't found a job in thirty years. "I can't find work," he said. "They just won't take me."

This familiar piece of fiction always reminded me of my childhood, when I had visited Aunt Blanche and Uncle Cliff for a week or two each summer. Every weekday morning, Uncle Cliff would walk out the door with a full dinner bucket and drive off toward the Maytag factory, where he stood on an assembly line for eight hours. Every evening he returned with an empty dinner bucket, which he rinsed out and placed on the counter to dry. Then I followed him into the screened porch at the back of the house, where he drank black coffee, smoked cigarettes, and told me about his day. "Patrick, I don't know what I'm going to do," he said. "I went everywhere in town, and I couldn't find work."

Sometimes, when Uncle Cliff was slow to initiate this nightly ritual, I overcame my natural shyness and took the lead. Sitting sideways on the chair next to his, I placed my elbows on the armrest, leaned toward him, and said, "Uncle Cliff, how did it go today? Did you find work?" The answer was always no, and we both treated this sad news with the utmost gravity.

Although they may not have known it, my father and my uncles habitually practiced the traditional humor of the American West, as the West was defined in the nineteenth century: that area of our republic that lies beyond the Appalachian Mountains. This form of humor depends for its effect on exaggeration and repetition. When asked about his health, my father would say that he was "just fair" or "doing poorly" or "near death." When asked about his crops, he would say, "Nothing will grow in these godforsaken hills." When asked about his children, he would say they were "penitentiary bound."

Visits to Uncle Emmett and my aunt in Ottumwa always began with the same ritualistic greeting. Father and Uncle Emmett would begin to stammer, scratch their heads, rub their chins, and stare at each other like primitive bipeds. Finally, after many false starts, they would both say, "The-the-the face is familiar, but-but-but I can't recall the name."

Once in the house, my aunt and my mother would flee to the kitchen, along with anyone else with delicate sensibilities, because Uncle Emmett habitually laced his stories with profane references to the name of our Heavenly Father. His stories were always set in the huge, cavernous packinghouse of John Morrell and Company, where he worked with thirty-five hundred other unfortunate souls, including a number of my other uncles. According to Uncle Emmett, this plant was filled with people with outlandish names, such as General Drop-cloth and Governor Herringbone, all of whom were constantly conspiring against each other in secret and ever-shifting alliances that, in their complexity, were not unlike those that led directly to the outbreak of World War I. Uncle Emmett was universally known as the Senator, a nickname that appeared in his obituary in the *Ottumwa Courier*. My father, who had also worked at the same packinghouse, played the straight man, asking penetrating questions that led my uncle into an even more outrageous narrative.

Uncle Emmett's appearance added an extra dimension to his humor. He was tall, large-boned, and knobby. His big nose complemented his large protruding ears. He always wore his pant legs short, in order, he said, "to keep my ankles cool." He moved with a slow, deliberate gait, suggesting that nothing on earth was more important than his own thoughts. The sad irony of his life was that he married one of my father's sisters, who, despite many excellent qualities, was entirely humorless.

═════════

I was blessed with a plentiful supply of aunts and uncles because my grandparents, Marion and Susan Hudgens Irelan, had produced twelve children, the first of whom was born in 1890. Grandma and Grandpa Irelan did not bring all these innocent lambs into the world merely because of God's injunction in the Book of Genesis, which says, "Be fruitful, and multiply," although they were no doubt familiar with that passage. They were, instead, simply following the nineteenth-century tradition of midwestern farm couples, among whom the justification for large families was primarily economic. The stress of childbearing, accompanied by the endless toil of house and garden work, also explains why farm women in the nineteenth century usually didn't live as long as farm men. Exactly the opposite is true today, now that huge expensive machines prepare the soil, plant the seeds, and harvest the crops, thereby making large families unnecessary.

But before the mechanization of the twentieth century, rural families depended for their survival on the help of several children to complete the multitude of daily tasks done by hand. In addition, the parents assumed that only about half of their children would live to adulthood. The other half would die of disease. Visit any country graveyard in the Middle West, and you will see the evidence of the high rate of infant mortality in the nineteenth century: small limestone markers bearing the names and dates of young children, often with a rosebud carved in the stone, along with the inscription "Born on Earth to Bud in Heaven." Monument works routinely kept a substantial supply of these stones on hand, certain they would not go unused.

But something remarkable happened in Grandma and Grandpa Irelan's family. Eleven of the twelve children actually did live to adulthood, and they and their cousins severely tested the limits of the public school system. While searching through our parents' effects, my sister and I found two of the little cards that country schoolteachers used to give the children as mementos at the end of each year. These cards included the name of the teacher, the names of all the students, and the names of the school's elected officers.

The cards we found had belonged to my father, who attended Buttontown School in Drakesville Township of Davis County. Emma Proctor, the teacher in 1913, listed twenty-eight students. Of these twenty-eight, nine bore the name Irelan. In other words, the Irelans constituted thirty-two percent of the school's students that year. The secretary of the school board in 1913 was Tom Irelan, my father's uncle. By 1915, Blanche Harshfield, the teacher that year, listed only seventeen students, but seven of them were named Irelan. Thus, in only two years, the percentage of Irelans in the school had grown to forty-one percent. Uncle Tom was still the secretary.

The only child in Grandma and Grandpa Irelan's family who didn't live to adulthood was Clayton, who died at the age of two from an accident, not a disease. He was suffering at the time from a mild childhood ailment, and the doctor came to see what could be done. He left a bottle of medicine and went on to make another call. When he reached the next house and opened his bag, he suddenly realized that what he had left for Clayton was not the intended medication, but a bottle of poison. My grandparents had a telephone, but by the time the doctor's call reached them, it was too late. Grandma Susie had given the child the poison, and there was no antidote. Clayton lingered for five weeks before he died.

In today's litigious society, such an event would set off an enormous lawsuit, but in 1911 people in Davis County, Iowa, didn't think that way. The doctor was horrified at what he had done, my grandparents knew that the poisoning was an accident, and everyone would have thought it immoral to use a child's death to obtain a financial reward.

All the other children lived well into adulthood. They were not as fruitful as my grandparents, but they did their best. After combining both my mother's family and my father's, my sister has calculated that she and I have thirty-five first cousins, not including those who died in infancy. I have never met some of these thirty-five and never will, because a number of them have already died.

In addition to the eagerness of my father's brothers and sisters to contribute to the earth's growing population, all of them shared one other characteristic: They were not a laconic bunch. Given the opportunity, they would talk your ear off. If you then made the mistake of turning around, they would talk your other ear off. Their minds contained a multitude of opinions, beliefs, and old family stories. They told these stories so often and with such enthusiasm that the children easily memorized them.

My father was no different from the rest. He held opinions on every subject and never resisted the urge to express them. He distrusted clergymen, lawyers, and bankers. He read something by Hemingway and declared it to be "nothing out of the ordinary." His report cards from Bloomfield High School indicate that he was an average student, and he often appeared to be completely anti-intellectual, yet he would frequently recite, from memory, long passages from Shakespeare; and when asked the meaning of a word, he would first define it and then give you its Latin derivation, when applicable, whether you wanted it or not. In this way, he demonstrated the advantages of an average high school education from the 1920s.

One of his deeply held and often-stated biases was that the invention of the tractor was the worst thing that had ever happened to the American farmer. "Tractors cost too much," he said. "They use expensive fuel. You have to maintain and repair them. And eventually they wear out. Then you have to borrow money to buy a new one that costs even more than the last one."

By contrast, he would explain, now gesturing broadly with both hands, "Horses don't cost as much. They eat hay and oats you can grow for yourself. And they rarely get sick or need to see the vet." But most important, he concluded triumphantly, although horses eventually grew old and died, they did something no tractor would ever do: "Every year the mares produce, at no cost whatsoever, new horses, which means you never have to borrow money to buy another one." Although the logic of this argument always struck me as entirely sound,

I never felt it would be polite to ask why we had a tractor instead of horses on our farm.

My father also claimed to believe in a number of superstitions, many of which I have never heard from anyone else. He often said, for example, "It's very bad luck to change the name of anything, especially a child." When my Aunt Lily gave birth to twins, a boy and a girl, she and Uncle Kenny briefly considered naming them John and Joan, but decided instead on Gene and Joan. My father saw in this a violation of his superstition against changing a child's name, and for the rest of his life, he always addressed Gene as "John," despite the protests of my mother. No one else seemed to mind, especially Gene himself, who developed a sense of humor strangely similar to my father's.

The curiosity in all this is that my father hated his own first and middle names — Curtis Glen — and refused to use them, except when signing legal documents. Even then, he preferred to use his initials if the law permitted it. He always signed his checks, for instance, as "C. G. Irelan."

I don't know why he disliked these names so much. I do know that when he went to Buttontown Grade School, someone gave him the nickname Pete, which he immediately seized with both hands and never let go. From that point on, when asked his name, he said, "Pete Irelan." If the situation required more formality, he said, "Peter Irelan."

By the time Pete graduated from Bloomfield High School, with his head full of Latin and Shakespeare, many of his schoolmates had no idea what his parents had originally named him. In subsequent years, the name Pete became even more firmly established. If someone addressed my father as "Curtis," he pretended not to hear. My mother called him "Pete" or "Daddy Pete." My sister and I called him "Daddy" or "Pete" or "Father." We called my mother "Mother," and after her children were born, Pete called her "Mother" also. Jane and I never used "Mom" or "Dad."

There *was* one person who could use the name Curtis and receive a polite response: Grandma Austa, my mother's mother. I think my father respected her nineteenth-century propriety, her hard work, and her fanatical devotion to her family. Besides that, she was just as stubborn as he was, and he knew it. If General Dropcloth or Governor Herringbone had called him "Curtis," he would have ignored them. The world is full of packinghouse politicians, and every four years their numbers increase dramatically as they take sudden interest in Iowa's venerable caucus system. But my grandmother was more formidable than any politician. She was a force that no one, not even my father, could ignore.

━━━━━━━━

As Uncle Cliff grew older, he became afflicted with multiple sclerosis, a disease that would lead slowly and painfully to his death. One summer day, years after my father had posed as the magazine salesman at Aunt Blanche and Uncle Cliff's house, I drove over to that same house in Newton. As always, Aunt Blanche's house was impeccably neat and clean. She habitually drew the praise of my mother and all my aunts for her housekeeping, even when she was working eight hours a day outside the home.

Aunt Blanche welcomed me with the same affection that she had when I was still a child. I don't know why she thought so highly of me. She must not have noticed my many faults.

She scurried around for a while, putting things in order that were already in order. She moved with a slight limp, the result of a collision with a drunk driver many years before when she and Uncle Cliff had just set out to visit my parents at their farm near Bloomfield. Finally, we went out to my car and drove to the hospital.

As soon as we entered Uncle Cliff's room, Aunt Blanche saw many things that displeased her. She didn't understand why an expensive hospital couldn't keep things in better order, and she set out to correct the faults that her sharp eyes immediately saw. All that I could see was Uncle Cliff, a hero of my vanished childhood, lying on his back, barely able to move.

"Patrick," he said, "I've been wanting to see you. How's Pete?"

My father had been dead for more than a year. "He's fine, Uncle Cliff," I said.

"Can he find work?"

"No, Uncle Cliff," I said. "He can't find a thing. He goes out every day, but no one will take him."

"That's just the way it is with me," he said. "You tell him I can't find anything either."

"Oh, Cliff," Aunt Blanche said, laughing at the ancient joke.

"I'll tell him the next time I see him," I said. "He told me to ask you if you were having any luck."

"Not a bit," Uncle Cliff said. "Not a bit. I haven't been able to find work in thirty years."

There was a long silence then while Uncle Cliff fought the pain. Aunt Blanche adjusted the pillows and helped him shift slightly in the bed. I stood there like a piece of granite, unable to move, unable to understand. Beyond the bed, the window admitted the ugly glare of the parking lot.

Finally, Uncle Cliff spoke again. "I just wish I could die," he said. "I just wish I could die."

"Now, Cliff," Aunt Blanche said, "don't say that. You don't mean that."

Uncle Cliff died six years later in 1984 at the age of seventy-nine. Aunt Blanche died on a Sunday morning in July of 1997 at the age of ninety-three, alert and lucid to the end.

After her funeral, my cousin Max pushed me into a car with his adult children for the ride to the graveyard. "In case you've forgotten," he told them, "this is my cousin Pat. Don't believe a word he says."

On a summer afternoon when I was five or six years old, Uncle Emmett drove down the lane to our house while I was at home with my mother. He had barely climbed out of the car before I was all over him. "Patrick," he said, "what are we ever going to do with you?" Mother came out of the house with a dish towel in her hand. I continued to pester Uncle Emmett, clinging to him like the hero he was. He was my uncle by marriage, the husband of one of my father's five sisters. Both he and my aunt were about fifteen years older than my parents.

Uncle Emmett didn't reject my affection or push me aside, but as my mother walked toward us, I could feel his body tighten. "Gerata," he said, his voice hoarse with emotion, "I almost hit her. By God, Gerata, when she started talking about my mother, I almost hit her."

I let go of my uncle's arm, but I didn't run away or pretend that I didn't see his distress. Our parents never taught my sister and me that life was free of pain or that if we believed in God our days would be filled with uninterrupted joy. My mother, who accepted the difficult task of our moral upbringing, knew the Book of Job as well as she knew the four gospels. "Let's go inside," Mother said. "We'll have a cup of coffee."

I followed my mother and uncle through the back door into the kitchen. She directed Uncle Emmett toward the chair at one end of the table where my father usually sat at mealtime. I lay down on my back on one of the rag rugs Mother used to hide the blemishes in the floor. I pulled my legs up until my feet were flat on the rug. I spread my arms out to the side. I lay there in the comfort and security of childhood, my body relaxed and free, while Uncle Emmett told my mother the story of his anger.

Mother made a fresh pot of coffee in her old metal dripolator, using the water I had pumped and carried into the kitchen half an hour before. Every visitor to our house said my mother made the best coffee in the world. She accepted this praise with polite dignity, never bothering to explain that the water from the well was the secret of her perfect coffee. My father, sister, and I all knew this secret, but we never revealed it either. As she busied herself with the water, the coffee, and the dripolator, she listened to my uncle. She said nothing but an occasional "oh dear" or similar interjection to acknowledge that she was following his narrative. At one point he uttered a profanity that he normally would not have spoken in her presence. Mother ignored it. She was treating a wounded man and had to make allowances. She finally sat down at the table while the hot water dripped through the coffee grounds and filled the little house with the aroma of my mother's perfect coffee.

She listened as Uncle Emmett continued his story, and when the coffee was ready, she poured a cup for him and another for herself. Then she sat back down. Both drank their coffee black. My uncle, a tall, lean, hardworking man, had diabetes. He put some of the artificial sweetener he always carried with him into his coffee, a sweetener that we now know is carcinogenic. But my uncle never got cancer from this or anything else. He suffered from a disease in my aunt's soul, and as it turned out, there was no cure for that disease but death itself. This disease expressed itself in a biting, critical meanness, directed most often, but not always, at my uncle. Why was my aunt the person she was? Why did she always treat my sister and me with sympathy and affection? How could she contain such contradictory traits as kindness and meanness in one personality? I stopped trying to answer those questions long ago, and even if I had found the answers, they would have solved nothing.

I lay there on the floor as Uncle Emmett began to talk himself out. I looked over at him. His hands seemed as big as five-pound hams, hams like those I would stuff into cans at the packinghouse in Ottumwa many years later. Attached to the right man, those hands could have easily killed my aunt; but I knew, even then, that Uncle Emmett would never hit her. He would come and talk to my mother instead.

As Uncle Emmett's emotion began to exhaust itself, my mother, slowly and with long pauses, began to talk. She blamed no one. She criticized no one. She talked about the past, of the many failures and rare successes of our large family, and of the hardships we had survived together. She reminded my uncle of what he had achieved, of the help he had given to friends and relatives at times when he himself was only a step less needy than they. She reminded him of his genius for storytelling and the pleasure it brought to so many people, even though she feared that her silly little boy might one day rupture himself while laughing and require the care of a doctor. Finally, Mother told Uncle Emmett what he already knew — that she, my father, my sister, and I had the greatest respect and affection for him and that that respect and affection would never die.

I held Uncle Emmett's huge hand as we walked out to his car. Before opening the door, he said, "Patrick, what are we ever going to do with you?"

I understand that colleges and universities now offer training in counseling, and I wish the counselors who emerge from these programs all the best in the difficult work they've chosen. My mother never took any courses in counseling. In fact, with the exception of a few night classes and some summer school courses in education, taken for the purpose of renewing her teaching certificate, she never attended college at all. So why did Uncle Emmett come to her that day? Why did so many others come to her? Where did she learn the magic that sent Uncle Emmett home that afternoon with the strength to eat his supper, sleep soundly, and return to the freezers in the packinghouse the next morning with the good humor that everyone he worked with would expect?

For once in my life, I can answer some of the questions that I continually ask myself. I know where my mother learned her magic: from her mother and my grandmother — Austa Fleming Hunter. My grandma's skill did not lie primarily in the field of counseling, a vocation greatly required in a disintegrating society such as ours, but largely unheard of in her time and place. She would extend sympathy to those who needed it, but she lived in an era and a place where an illness was more likely to be physical than emotional. Everyone in the agrarian community where she lived most of her life struggled to survive every year, but no one had to fear street gangs or repeatedly risk his or her life on the Stevenson Expressway. All the familiar causes of anxiety in our country today did not exist in and around Ash Grove, Iowa, during my grandmother's life there.

I have been told that many people now go to stores to buy expensive herbal remedies for the countless afflictions that plague humankind. Grandma Austa did not buy herbs at stores. When someone came to her with an ailment that she knew she could treat, she would go into the woods and meadows to find the herb or herbs she needed. Although she was devoutly religious, Grandma never claimed that she could improve someone's health through direct appeals to God. She would comfort and console the sick and discouraged, but she left spiritual matters to the clergy. Nothing dismayed her more than "faith healers" who claimed that they had immediate access to the Almighty and could cure a disease in return for regular contributions.

My grandmother was born in Ash Grove, Iowa, on January 11, 1879, and grew up as a child of the Iowa frontier. She remembered that when she was a little girl, Indians would occasionally come to the house to trade with her parents, John and Susan Adcock Fleming. The Indians avoided some houses because experience had taught them that the whites who lived there would try to cheat them. But they always stopped at the Fleming homestead because they had learned from previous visits that they would be invited into the house and treated as equals. Both the Indians and Grandma's parents bargained vigorously, but neither side would lie or resort to trickery.

The Indians who came to the house fascinated my grandmother. She noted their dignity and propriety, and she desperately wanted to know what they knew about the natural world around them. When a question about a particular plant formed in her mind and the moment was right, she would ask her parents whether they could ask the Indians a question for her. Her parents never refused to ask the question, and Grandma never forgot the answer. In this manner, she gradually acquired a small body of knowledge about the unfamiliar wild plants that grew in abundance on her parents' farm.

To the knowledge she acquired from these Indians, my grandmother added the more extensive understanding of familiar health-giving plants handed down to her from generations of her own family. By the time she finished grade school and became a young woman, Grandma had become the master of her environment. She had also become beautiful. A family portrait taken at that time reveals a firm chin and lovely neck. Her delicate nose and dark-blue eyes must have caught the attention of all the young men in the neighborhood. She never cut her brown hair, but kept it tied up in an elaborate bun. She was both beautiful and intelligent, and no man was ever more fortunate than Laris Hunter, my grandfather, who married Grandma Austa on New Year's Day of 1901, the first day of a century that would prove the worst of what human beings can do.

It sometimes causes me a touch of pain when I find myself writing that one of my ancestors was especially attractive, for precious little of

The John and Susan Adcock Fleming family in the late 1890s. Wray, the youngest child, sits in front. The second row includes (l–r) Sylvia, Susan, John, and Clarence. Standing in the third row are Bessie, Barton, Austa, and Gilford. Photograph courtesy of Marsha and Stewart Hunter.

that attractiveness ever filtered down to me. If this is the way the laws of genetics work, I would have liked an occasional violation of the law.

In addition to her other skills, Grandma was a midwife. My mother recalled the countless nights when someone would knock at the door at any hour. Without complaint, Grandma rose, dressed, and went out into the darkness, where a nervous father-to-be would be waiting to help her into the buggy. The next morning, she would return and say only that this or that family had a new baby.

Grandma's knowledge and wisdom always astounded me. When I was a little boy, I believed that she had memorized the entire King James Version of the Bible. I now know that that was unlikely. She couldn't have memorized more than eighty or ninety percent. Grandma spoke her own language of biblical quotations and nineteenth-century American English, and she knew when and how to employ this personal language. She would not abide an unkind word spoken about anyone she knew. If someone foolishly made such a statement in her presence, she would rebut the criticism with an appropriate quotation from the Bible, or by saying something complimentary about the individual criticized, or by doing both. And God help the ignorant soul who ever spoke a word of criticism about anyone in Grandma's family. If you were related to her by blood or marriage, she would brook no insult to your character, your behavior, your appearance, or anything else. Such an insult would summon long passages from the Bible and a detailed refutation of the insult.

As far as I know, Grandma Austa had only one fault: She never stopped working, even after moving off the farm. I learned when quite young that talking to Grandma required constant movement both inside and outside her house in Ottumwa — in the kitchen, in the garden, in the yard, in the apartment on the second floor, in the basement with its deplorable plumbing, and in any other place that her tireless energy sent her. She never refused to answer the questions I asked her, no matter how painful the subject, because she could not rebuff her grandchild and she could not lie. Moreover, she approved of my interest in our family and its long history. I learned all this about my grandma, and I now confess that I took advantage of her because of my selfish desire to know everything she knew, despite the fact that I could never have learned in a hundred lifetimes all that she could teach me.

Grandma Austa possessed a great storehouse of folk wisdom and common sense that she had collected like the herbs from the meadows. The theme she continually returned to, as I followed her about, was that to criticize someone else actually amounted to criticizing yourself, for it revealed your own lack of self-respect. She also thought the doctrine of original sin to be a great pile of nonsense. "Adam sinned only for himself," she said. "The rest of us have to commit our own sins, if that's what we're determined to do." She quickly followed this by advising me against sinful behavior, although at my young age I had no clear idea of what sinfulness involved.

"What *is* sin, Grandma?" I asked.

"It's doing something very bad, Sweetheart," she said, "something God wouldn't want you to do."

"What kinds of things?"

"Things like stealing something or killing someone, very bad things." She wisely ignored the sin of adultery, which would have led to more questions that I'm sure Grandma did not want to discuss with a five-year-old grandson.

Even so, I then had a clearer understanding of the nature of sin, although I couldn't stop to reflect on it because Grandma would have already started up the stairs or down the stairs, and I had to keep up to avoid missing something, even if I didn't know entirely what it meant. "Human beings are weak, Patrick," she said. "That's why you must always remain faithful to your family. If you ever really need help, you can be sure of no one but your family." I had never noticed anything seriously wrong with my family, so I found this advice easy to follow. In fact, I don't think I ever disagreed with anything Grandma told me, including what she said one day while dusting off the piano: "If you're proud of how good looking you are, you should throw away your mirror."

From a tiny cell somewhere in my brain, with dendrites still intact and synapses still sparkling, I can summon at will a vivid memory of the day, when at the age of four, for the only time in my life, I saw my grandmother let down her gray-brown hair to brush it. It reached all the way to her waist. She turned from the mirror and smiled at me where I sat in a rocking chair. "You didn't know Grandma had such long hair, did you, Patrick?"

"No, Grandma," I said. "How long did it take to grow that far?"

"Sixty-eight years," she said, still smiling.

Sixty-eight surpassed the limits of my numerical powers at that time. Anything higher than ten went into an unused cerebral file that reached from eleven to infinity. But it didn't make any difference to me then. I knew at that moment that I would understand sixty-eight someday and that Grandma would always be there when I needed her.

Twenty-three years later, in 1970, five of her other grandsons and I bore Grandmother Austa Fleming Hunter's casket to the grave. She lies beside my grandfather at Hopewell, the country graveyard only a short distance north of the farm the Hunter family has owned for more than 125 years, the farm where she and Grandpa raised their family. Around her lie the graves of her children and their faithful spouses, and where, with the passage of time, her grandchildren will follow her home.

THE LANDSCAPE

When the white pioneers arrived in Davis County in the 1840s and 1850s, they saw that the northern half of the county was hilly and heavily wooded and that the southern half was flatter and possessed relatively few trees. The hilliness of the northern half resulted from about five hundred thousand years of the meandering of a little stream called Soap Creek, which flows from west to east and empties into the Des Moines River. Because the pioneers needed wood for buildings, fences, and fuel, the first to arrive settled in the northern half of the county. The latecomers settled in the south.

What none of these people could have known was that the flatter land in the southern half of the county was more fertile than the hilly land in the north, that millions of pine logs in rafts an acre or more in size would soon come floating down the Mississippi River from Minnesota and Wisconsin, that Joseph Glidden would invent barbed wire in De Kalb, Illinois, in 1873, and that many counties in the southern half of Iowa contained shallow deposits of coal almost anywhere you wanted to start digging.

So the pioneers didn't really need all those trees. Sawmills in Dubuque, Clinton, Davenport, Muscatine, and Burlington soon began cutting the pine logs into lumber and shipping it west on newly built railroads, where it would be used to construct houses and other buildings. Coal mines appeared throughout southern Iowa and began producing inexpensive fuel that quickly replaced wood. And barbed wire soon made wooden fences obsolete.

In a pattern repeated in much of the Middle West, the first to arrive got the best trees, and the last to arrive got the best land. I regret to inform you that my ancestors, eager and energetic to a fault, were among the first to arrive. They realized too late that the trees hindered cultivation and offered little of value in return. Moreover, the land was too hilly, and the soil was poor.

My father, who reached his prime a century later, understood the error his ancestors had made, and as a result he developed a hatred of trees that bordered on the pathological. Consequently, when I grew old enough, he sent me forth with a double-bladed ax each summer to murder every sapling that threatened to become a tree. I left the trees themselves alone, because they provided shade for the cattle. I enjoyed this work because it afforded me with long periods of solitude, during which I allowed my mind to engage in the uninterrupted dreaminess essential to the development of an adolescent child's imagination. My efforts also pleased my father, who responded with generous praise.

In addition to their other faults, trees provided an inferior means of heating a house when easier methods arrived. When my grandfather Hunter needed fuel, he didn't chop down a tree. He simply hitched his team to a wagon and went to a coal mine, where the workers loaded the wagon for him. My parents heated our farmhouse with coal during my entire childhood, although the coal company brought it to us in a truck and dumped it in a pile about twenty yards behind the house. Twice each winter day, I dutifully walked out to this pile, filled two coal buckets, and carried them into the house. I don't know how much a bucket of coal weighs, but it's considerably more than a bucket of marshmallows. A foot or two of snow atop the coal pile made the task even more complicated.

According to historian Dorothy Schwieder, coal mining in Iowa reached its peak in 1925, when 354 mines employed more than eleven thousand miners. John L. Lewis, who would eventually become president of the United Mine Workers of America, was born in a coal camp near Albia, Iowa, in 1880. The coal industry declined when the railroads switched from steam locomotives to diesel and when people began heating their houses with natural gas instead of coal. At present, not a single coal mine remains in operation in Iowa. The last mine closed only a few years ago. It employed one miner, who used the best mining machines and safety equipment. The *Des Moines Register* sent a reporter out to interview that miner. The man said he liked his job because the temperature down in the mine was always fifty-five degrees, and he felt most comfortable working in those conditions. I don't know where that man is today, but I hope he has a good job where it's always fifty-five degrees.

The last of the pioneers to arrive in Iowa settled in the northern part of the state. They also wanted trees, but missed their chance. Most of

Iowa consisted of gently rolling tall-grass prairie, with forested hills along the rivers and streams. There were notable exceptions to this generalization, especially the spectacular cliffs, deep valleys, and hardwood forests of northeast Iowa. But one factor, glaciation, made a large expanse of northern Iowa different from the south. The last glacier, the Wisconsinan, to reach what would become the state of Iowa made its southernmost advance about fourteen thousand years ago. It covered the north central part of the state, known by geologists today as the Des Moines Lobe, making that region geologically much younger than southern Iowa. As a result, when the pioneers arrived, the rivers and streams in much of the north had not yet carved out the kinds of hills and valleys found in poor but scenic areas farther south, areas like those in Davis County where timber covers much of the landscape.

If you would like to see how far south the last glacier extended, go to the grounds of the State Capitol in Des Moines and open your eyes. The exterior of that building — with its central gold-leaf dome and four smaller domes, one at each corner of the building — was constructed primarily of Iowa granite, sandstone, and, finally, limestone from that vast sarcophagus of the aquatic creatures of ancient inland seas. The Capitol sits on a knoll formed by glacial debris, or drift, left behind when the average temperature rose and the glacier began to melt.

More evidence of the last glacier's southernmost advance can be seen in the course of the Raccoon River, which enters the city of Des Moines from the west and empties into the Des Moines River at about the center of town. The Wisconsinan glacier actually forced the Raccoon River southward into its present channel, which now lies along the edge of the former ice sheet. I know these facts about the Wisconsinan glacier because I called Jean Prior, a senior research geologist with the Iowa Department of Natural Resources, and she patiently explained them to me.

And now I'm going to take a great leap into the geological past, for which Ms. Prior is entirely innocent. If you would like a dramatic sense of the long-departed Wisconsinan glacier, drive west down the hill from the State Capitol, cross the Des Moines River, turn left, go about five blocks to Riverside Park, and find a parking place. Get out of your car, and you will find yourself standing in a spot that is, geologically speaking, about fourteen thousand years old.

Next, walk south across the Raccoon River on the First Street Bridge, go a few more yards beyond the levee, and look around. By merely crossing that bridge, you will find yourself standing in a place that is as much as five hundred thousand years old, because that is how long it has been since a glacial stage, the Pre-Illinoian, has reached that far south in what is now Iowa, ultimately halting in the northern half of Missouri.

Fans of minor league baseball, one of whom I am, may want to note that Sec Taylor Stadium, the home of the Iowa Cubs, sits in Riverside Park at about the distance of a Mickey Mantle home run from the confluence of the Des Moines and Raccoon rivers. Although most of us think of the Ice Age as over and done with, many geologists believe that it is far from being over and that we are now living in a period of inter-glacial warmth. If these geologists are correct, the Iowa Cubs may someday have to move their stadium.

━━━━━━━━

In addition to the scarcity of trees in northern Iowa, the pioneers also had to confront an abundance of wetlands left in the wake of the last glacier. Although these broad, shallow pools of water were ecological marvels, the Germans, Swedes, Norwegians, Irish, Bohemians, Dutch, native-born Americans, and many other ethnic groups who settled in northern Iowa found that the wetlands made the ground they covered impossible to cultivate. They could not plow a field that had six inches of water standing in it. The pioneers saw no alternative. They had to be-gin the laborious task of digging drainage ditches by hand.

When they began to plow the land, they discovered the fertile black topsoil that the wetlands and tall grasses had created during the four-teen thousand years since the retreat of the last glacier. But it was not until they began to dig wells or other deep excavations that they real-ized what they had acquired by arriving late.

After turning over the first two or three shovels of dirt, they were un-doubtedly pleased to see that the topsoil remained as black as coal. In fact, the topsoil often reached ten or twelve inches in depth, which was definitely not the case in Ireland, Sweden, Bohemia, or Pennsylvania. Beneath this beautiful black dirt, they found other soils that, while not as pleasing to the eye as topsoil, were quite fertile. When the pioneers reached a depth of two or three feet, I would imagine that they started to lose all interest in the scarcity of trees. At four feet, they could be for-given if they began to doubt the evidence of their senses.

But at about six feet — when the soil finally gave out and sand, gravel, or something else emerged — they had to acknowledge that what they saw before them was not a delusion. These people — many of whom had recently crossed a vast ocean in wet, stinking, rat-infested ships — had stumbled upon a miracle. Almost by accident, they had taken possession of some of the most fertile soil in the world. They received this reward for arriving late, and those of us from the clay hills of southern Iowa have regretted the promptness of our ancestors ever since.

———

When the pioneers began moving into the Middle West, they brought with them their livestock, their horses or oxen, their tools and farm equipment, their clothing, their furniture, their pianos, and a great deal more, including their accents — their different ways of pronouncing nineteenth-century American English. The fact that their descendants presently living in the Middle West speak one of two major dialects is, in large part, a direct result of the migration patterns that their ancestors followed. The ancestors of the people in central Iowa, for example, tended to follow a route from Pennsylvania to northern Ohio, northern Indiana, northern Illinois, and finally to Iowa. These migrations often took two or more generations.

By contrast, the forebears of the people of Missouri tended to follow a route from Kentucky or West Virginia through southern Ohio, southern Indiana, southern Illinois, and into Missouri. Like their neighbors in Iowa, these pioneers did not just get up one morning and head west with no particular destination in mind. In many cases, they already had friends or relatives living in the area they set off for. All this explains why the people of the Middle West have two different accents today. Their ancestors planted those accents on the landscapes they inhabited, and the accents have remained exceptionally stable ever since. Immigrants who came directly to the Middle West from European countries where English was not spoken acquired the accents of their English-speaking neighbors as they and their children learned American English.

If you were to look at a map of the United States as divided into various regions by a dialectologist, you would see that a horizontal line divides the Middle West into two sections. The northern section is called the north central region, and the southern section is called the central midland region. In each of these regions, the people speak a distinct dialect of American English.

A professional dialectologist could explain all this more accurately and in much greater detail, but I am not a professional dialectologist and do not have at the moment the six or seven years it would take to become one. But I can hear as well as the average person, and my ears tell me that in the north central region, most people speak English with a flat midwestern accent. This accent does not have any characteristics that make it stand out from the speech of the rest of the country. When television networks go in search of men and women to report the news, they head for this part of the country first. Listen to the evening news on one of the major networks, if you can stand the content and commercials, and you will undoubtedly hear the accent of the north central region spoken by many or most of the reporters.

You will also hear this accent spoken throughout large portions of California, partly because during the 1930s and 1940s tens of thousands of people from the upper Midwest decided they could no longer endure winters in which temperatures often dropped to twenty below zero and summers in which temperatures of one hundred degrees seemed as common as mosquitoes. The extremes of this weather, especially in Iowa and Nebraska, along with the ruinous effects of the Great Depression, finally led these people to pack their bags, take the train to California, and return to the Middle West only for the funerals of those who stayed behind. So many Iowans moved to southern California during this period that they used to hold annual Iowa Picnics attended by thousands of people, although that tradition, like a sad number of the people who started it, has now died.

Unlike the flat accent heard in the north central region, the speech of the central midland region does have a characteristic sound that distinguishes it from the spoken language of the rest of the country. Most people in this region speak with an easily recognized nasal twang. This twang in no way resembles a southern drawl and should not be confused with it. If you want to hear this nasal twang in its unadulterated form, catch the next train to central Missouri, go to a small rural town, order something to eat in a local café, and start listening. You will hear the unmistakable sound of the central midland twang.

When one becomes familiar with the two distinct dialects of the Middle West, a logical question often follows. If you were to travel through the Midwest from south to north, where would the twang of the central midland region give way to the flat generic speech of the north central region? If we return to the dialectologist's map, we find that this change occurs along an east-west line that passes through the southernmost part of the state of Iowa, which includes Davis County, the home of generations of my family. In Missouri, the speech of the central midland is called a "Missouri twang." But in Iowa we are far too proud of our state to use this term. Instead, we call it a "southern Iowa twang." The sound is the same, but the name is different, although the farther south you go in Missouri, the more pronounced the twang becomes, until it disappears into the Ozark Mountains of southern Missouri and northern Arkansas and emerges farther south transformed into the southern dialect.

The dialectologist's map could lead some innocent soul to conclude that a magic line indicates exactly where the central midland accent suddenly gives way to the north central accent. The dialectologist knows that this is not true and that the line is only an approximation. I know that the line is only an approximation because I grew up where the line appears on the map and can testify that the line passes directly through counties, towns, schools, sale barns, and houses. I know a family in which the three youngest children speak with the southern Iowa twang and the three oldest children do not.

I cannot explain this phenomenon and paid little attention to it until I reached adulthood and left Davis County for an extended period of quixotic adventures farther north. When I returned, I heard more clearly than before the distinct variation in speech along the magic line. Since then, I have discovered that some people who have lived in Davis County for their entire lives are unaware of the variation in speech that exists all around them. Most children are completely oblivious to the magic line.

My father spoke with the north central accent, but he also possessed a good ear for language and the skill of mimicry. Because some people from farther north mistakenly believe that the southern Iowa twang is an indication of ignorance, Pete often adopted this accent when negotiating the sale of antiques or other objects with these misguided individuals. He never tried this with cattle traders. They could see a worthless steer for what it was regardless of what accent you used to talk about it. But the trick often worked to his advantage with other people, probably because the buyers thought my father too ignorant to realize that the objects under consideration were worth more than he knew. In fact, he knew exactly what they were worth and sold them for more than that amount.

One might think Pete's tactics unscrupulous, but I always thought them entirely justified. He never lied to anyone. He just changed the way he spoke, and that caused some people to think that he was stupid. They walked away with their overpriced baubles and didn't even try to hide the smug looks on their faces. By contrast, Pete always remained extremely polite. He waited until the victims were out of earshot. Then he laughed until his face turned red. Even today, decades later, every time I see someone puffed up with conceit, I swear that I can hear my father laughing.

THELMA

As a young woman, Aunt Thelma Hunter's most striking characteristic was her physical beauty. She may even have been as beautiful as her mother, my grandmother Austa. The evidence for these claims resides in a family portrait taken by the Warner Studio in Bloomfield sometime in 1928, when Aunt Thelma was twenty-three years old. Grandpa, Grandma, and Uncle Kenny are sitting in front from left to right. Aunt Dottla, Aunt Thelma, and my mother stand behind them. The photographer has placed his brightest lamp on his left side and his secondary lamp on his right, thereby illuminating most strongly the right side of each subject's face. This works best for the three girls, but tends to obscure the left side of those seated in the front row. The photographer could have corrected this problem with a simple adjustment of the lamp on his left side, but he obviously chose not to do this.

Poor Grandpa looks like the victim of malicious hatchet lighting, which obliterates the left side of his face and leaves his right side in a shadow. Grandma and Uncle Kenny fare better, but the viewer's eye inevitably focuses on Aunt Thelma, whose unsmiling face reduces the other subjects to a supporting cast. The light falls perfectly on a face that tempts her sentimental nephew to describe it as sublime. It appears that the photographer has forgotten the other subjects altogether and employed all his skill to capture that vision of Aunt Thelma. My dear mother, standing on Aunt Thelma's left, is even slightly out of focus.

Aunt Thelma seems to possess a haughty beauty. Her chin is slightly elevated. Her eyes have focused on something just to the left of the camera, as if she has no interest in the photographer and the image he will produce. Her short, naturally curly hair — brown with a red tint that the black-and-white photo cannot reveal — provides an ideal frame for her slender nose, elegant chin, and all the other features of her perfectly symmetrical face. Her throat and neck tempt me to compare them with the marble statue of a great sculptor, except that no sculptor has ever been that good. Aunt Thelma appears so confident of her beauty that she may decide to ignore forever this portrait after the tiresome photographer has finally produced it in the darkroom.

But the photographer has created an illusion. The image lies. Although Aunt Thelma was beautiful, she was never haughty. She lacked confidence in all her physical and intellectual gifts. She was timid, unassertive, and fearful. And when my grandfather later told the young man she loved that he would not permit Aunt Thelma to marry him, she lacked the courage to defy her father and marry the man anyway.

Grandpa Laris Hunter wanted one of his three daughters to remain at home with Grandma and him to care for them in their old age. He chose Aunt Thelma for this duty, and although he may never have said why, everyone in the family knew why. If he had denied my mother permission to marry, she would have smiled, nodded politely, and gone off with my father to select their wedding rings. If he had forbidden my aunt Dottla to marry, her response would have been more vigorous and direct, for Aunt Dottla possessed great self-confidence and rarely hesitated to say what was on her mind.

Grandpa chose Aunt Thelma because he knew that only she would obey him. I do not mean to condemn my grandfather. He worked as hard as any man ever did to support his family. He sacrificed his own comfort to ensure that his children would receive the best education they could, and I would never claim the right to criticize him or any of my other grandparents. They gave life itself to all of us who followed them into this world.

How could I criticize the grandfather who held me on his lap and made me laugh, who taught me how to tell time when I was five years old, thereby unlocking the greatest of all mysteries. "What time is it, Patrick?" he said to me one day as he sat in his rocking chair in the parlor.

"I don't know, Grandpa," I said from the front room. "I don't know how to tell time."

"What?" he said. "Don't know how to tell time? A great big boy like you?" He climbed out of his rocking chair and walked into the front room, where an antique clock stood atop the piano. He pointed at the minute hand. He pointed at the hour hand. He began to talk. Five minutes later I knew how to tell time, and as a bonus I knew every Roman numeral from one to twelve. I remember him during those five minutes more vividly than at any other time in my life: his cigarette-stained

The Warner Studio in Bloomfield, Iowa, produced this portrait of the Laris and Austa Fleming Hunter family in 1928. Laris, Austa, and Kenneth (l–r) are seated in front. Dottla, Thelma, and Gerata (l–r) stand in back. Author's collection.

white mustache, his brilliant eyes, his compelling baritone voice. I could never criticize this man, but in all honesty, the only way I can defend his decision regarding my beautiful aunt Thelma is to point out the obvious fact that his era was different from ours, and I see precious little evidence that our era is better.

I don't know the name of the man who fell in love with Aunt Thelma and asked her to marry him, and I have no idea what happened to him after his failed courtship. My mother never told me these details. But I do know that that man was one of the unluckiest men on earth, for in addition to the beauty that Aunt Thelma possessed, she was also intelligent, loving, and kind. Unless I am badly mistaken, she would have been an excellent wife and mother. And because Aunt Thelma always displayed good judgment and never rushed into anything, I have to assume that the nameless young man probably would have made an excellent husband and father. I don't see a great number of couples like that nowadays, and I don't know why, but it isn't because fathers won't let their daughters marry.

———

After giving up the prospect of marriage, Aunt Thelma continued to teach grade school, just as she had since her high-school graduation. And over a period of many summers, she earned her bachelor's degree from Iowa State Teachers College in Cedar Falls and her master's degree from Drake University in Des Moines. After teaching in many different schools she finally settled in Ottumwa, where she taught fourth grade at Irving Elementary School until she retired. Altogether, she taught for forty-five years. Irving School, a large, three-story brick structure built in the Gothic style, stood on the south side of town at a spot known as "the Five Corners." I remember riding past that school with my mother many times when I was a little boy. It never failed to impress me that my aunt Thelma taught in such a grand building. But don't look for Irving School today. All you'll find in that spot is a fast-food joint.

As it turned out, Grandpa and Grandma did need Aunt Thelma's help. When Grandpa became an invalid with the asthma that would eventually kill him, Aunt Thelma bought the house on Glenwood Avenue in Ottumwa where she and my grandparents lived for the rest of their lives. Grandma remained healthy long into old age, and she provided all the personal care that Grandpa needed. But Aunt Thelma paid the bills. As a teacher, Aunt Thelma was so conscientious that my mother sometimes chided her for the long hours she spent grading assignments during the evenings and weekends. "You don't have to grade every piece of paper they turn in," Mother would say.

"Oh, if I tell the children to do an assignment, I have to grade it," Aunt Thelma said, "or they'll think the assignments aren't important."

In order to help Aunt Thelma, my mother often volunteered my services for yard work and other chores when I was a boy. I sometimes thought my mother was too generous with my services, but I kept those thoughts to myself and obediently did the work, just as Aunt Thelma would have done as a child. Her house had a small lawn, so I could mow it with the push mower without collapsing from exhaustion.

Aunt Thelma also needed to have the bushes trimmed. With this task, I met with less success. Aunt Thelma explained exactly how to trim each bush. Because of her teaching skills, she could explain everything clearly. I understood her instructions, but I ran into trouble when trying to follow them. I saw the perfectly trimmed bush in my mind but couldn't create it in the real world. If I trimmed too little, Aunt Thelma would say, "I think you need to take off a bit more," and I would do as she said. If I trimmed too much, Aunt Thelma would also point out that imperfection, but I could do nothing to remedy the problem except state the obvious, which was that the bush would grow back. On those occasions, Aunt Thelma allowed herself to look at me with a hint of reproach, just as she must have allowed herself to look at a student who failed to follow her well-stated instructions. But she never belittled my efforts. As a teacher, she knew the damage that that might cause to my adolescent personality. My personality was none too splendid anyway, and Aunt Thelma wanted to encourage me despite my trouble with bushes.

My mother also volunteered my help when Aunt Thelma needed to have her car washed, and this need arose when the first touch of dirt appeared on her frequently serviced and perfectly maintained four-door Ford sedan. Aunt Thelma had learned that unless the underside of each fender was kept clean, the metal would begin to rust from beneath and eventually holes would appear in the fenders. To combat this problem, she had acquired an attachment for the end of her garden hose that would allow a healthy though clumsy boy such as myself to thoroughly clean the undersides of the fenders. Aunt Thelma always supervised this part of the job to ensure that I did it correctly. I would attack each fender and when finished would ask if I should next wash the car's exterior. Without bending down to inspect my work, which would have been unladylike, Aunt Thelma said, "I think you need to do the fenders again."

My aunt Thelma had somehow acquired the ability to see through fenders, and she knew they needed to be cleaned again. She was entirely correct, but I remain mystified to this day by the capacity of her eyes to penetrate solid steel. I would attack the undersides of the fenders a second time and ask again if I should now wash the outside of the car. By means of her omnipotent eyesight, Aunt Thelma concluded that I should "just do the fenders one more time." I went at it again and then finally proceeded to wash the car's exterior. Unlike the trimming of bushes, this task required no special skills or eye-hand coordination and I made quick work of it to the complete satisfaction of Aunt Thelma. Although I didn't care too much for the underbody work, I couldn't help noticing, as the years passed, the total absence of holes in the Ford's fenders.

Because she had no children of her own, Aunt Thelma paid special attention to her nieces and nephews. One day long after I had grown up and left home, I went to visit my mother when Aunt Thelma happened to be there. My old Pontiac was literally falling apart, and I didn't see how it could make it through another winter. Quite out of the blue, without being asked, Aunt Thelma said, "Pat, if you can find a good used car, I could lend you the money to buy it."

"Thank you, Aunt Thelma," I said after recovering from the surprise of this sudden offer. In my selfishness, it later occurred to me that all that yard mowing and bush trimming hadn't been too much trouble after all. I looked around, found a used car that seemed to run well, haggled awhile with the salesman, and reported back to Aunt Thelma, who immediately wrote a check to the car dealer in the amount of twenty-one hundred dollars. I paid her back at the rate of seventy dollars a month, and despite my protests, she refused to accept any interest on the loan.

I drove that car for years, in all kinds of weather, for both short trips and long, with babies securely strapped into their baby seats and adults with seat belts securely engaged. The car never found itself parked in a garage. I owned a garage, but it required the strength of an Olympic weight lifter to open and close the door. So I always parked the car on the street. The engine continued to run well and might have lasted for two hundred thousand miles or more. But after about ten years, the car became something of an embarrassment. With typical abandon, I had failed to remember one of Aunt Thelma's most valuable lessons from my childhood, and it was now too late to correct the oversight. And as you have guessed, every fender was full of holes.

HEROES

Almost every family can claim some hero or heroine from the mythic past to whom the family can return for consolation during hard times. If no such hero exists, some clever relative can invent one. If one does exist, everyone can help exaggerate his or her accomplishments to suit the needs of the day. In the Irelan family, the heroes to whom we turn for inspiration are William and Elizabeth Jane Fullerton Irelan, my great-grandparents.

William Irelan, the descendant of impoverished immigrants, was born in Ohio in 1840. His parents could neither read nor write. Because of the advent of free public education, William would learn reading, writing, and a great deal more. At the age of thirteen, he moved to Iowa with his parents and sister, where the family purchased a farm. He attended grade school in both Ohio and Iowa and demonstrated at an early age a gift for mechanics and inventiveness.

When William was nineteen, his father died, leaving him to provide for his mother and sister. Later that year, he added another member to the family by marrying Elizabeth Jane Fullerton three days before Christmas in 1859.

Elizabeth Jane was also a native of Ohio. Born in 1842, she moved to Iowa with her parents, brothers, and sisters in the early 1850s. Like William she attended school in both Ohio and Iowa. During the Civil War, three of her brothers volunteered. Only one returned alive.

But my great-grandfather William Irelan did not volunteer. Farm families rarely sent all their young men off to war. Some had to stay home to provide for those who could not provide entirely for themselves. William had his mother, his young sister, and his wife to provide for, but had no brothers at all. In the laudatory prose of the nineteenth century, the 1882 *History of Davis County, Iowa* reports of William that

> being in reduced circumstances he had a hard time, but being energetic, he succeeded. At that time [1859] his capital consisted of one horse, one cow, two sheep, and one pig. Not getting along very well

on the farm and being a natural mechanic, he built a shop and did jobbing of all kinds, and in the winter of 1868, he bought a half interest in a saw mill, which he ran with success for one year, when he sold out and bought a mill of his own.

But that was only the beginning. The article goes on to say that in the years from 1877 to 1879, he invented and patented three separate types of steel-truss bridges, formed a bridge-building company, and began erecting bridges for railroads and local governments. "He purchased a farm of 349 acres of the best improved land in the township [Marion], with good buildings, where he now lives," the *History* records. While engaged in these energetic projects, he continued to run his saw-mill and opened a combination lumberyard and hardware store in Drakesville.

William and Elizabeth Jane were equally productive on the domestic front. Elizabeth gave birth to nine children, seven of whom lived well into adulthood. Of the five boys who survived childhood, one ran the lumberyard, three became farmers, and one became a doctor. The two daughters married and raised families of their own.

In a photograph of the family taken when all the surviving children had reached adulthood, William and Elizabeth Jane are seated next to their two daughters. Both of the girls look as proper as humanly possible.

The five boys are standing behind their parents and sisters. Charles, the one who ran the lumberyard, appears decidedly bookish and is the only person in the photograph wearing eyeglasses. He is also the only boy who is not sporting a mustache. All the boys look quite serious, except for my grandfather Marion, who has turned slightly to the side and appears to be gazing dreamily at something in the distance. He looks like a man who has never had a worry in his life and never will.

By contrast, Great-Grandmother Elizabeth Jane looks eager to get back to work. Great-Grandfather William is wearing a full beard and has the confident expression of a man who can build bridges or anything else he wants to. People who see photographs of William tell me I look very much like him. But there, I regret, all similarity ends. I have little ambition, less money, and could not build a birdhouse in which any sparrow would spend a minute.

Elizabeth Jane died in 1917 at the age of seventy-four. Her obituary in the *Bloomfield Democrat* declared that she had "lived a consistent

William and Elizabeth Jane Fullerton Irelan sit with their children, circa 1890s.
Daughters Meta and Alice (l–r) sit beside their parents. Sons Charles, George,
Marion, Henry, and Thomas stand behind their parents and sisters. Photograph
courtesy of Jeanne and Max Irelan.

Christian life every day as long as she lived." It went on to say, "She, all her life long, sacrificed for her family."

Because of her devotion to her children, her generosity to her friends and neighbors, her unshakable religious faith, and her tireless labor, Elizabeth Jane occupies a place of high regard in the Irelan family. This respect has shown itself most clearly in the use that subsequent generations have made of the names Jane and Elizabeth. The examples that immediately come to mind are my aunt Jane, my sister Jane, two nieces with the middle name Jane, and my own daughters — Emily Jane and Claire Elizabeth.

William died in 1925 at the age of eighty-four. His obituary in the *Bloomfield Democrat* described him as a "Drakesville pioneer." It also stated that, in addition to his seven surviving children, he left forty-six grandchildren and twenty-one great-grandchildren.

But to understand the place of William and Elizabeth Jane in the Irelan psyche, one has to get back to the crucial issue — money. The

1882 *History of Davis County, Iowa* quoted earlier concludes its description of William: "Mr. I. is one of the wealthiest men in Davis County, honored and respected by all who know him."

Honor and respect have their place, but what quickens the Irelan pulse in the present era is the thought of all that money. And this raises an inevitable question: How much money did William and Elizabeth Jane have? At a family reunion many years ago, one of my uncles said, "Whenever one of their children got married, they gave the couple ten thousand dollars." Another uncle immediately disputed this figure. "No, I think they gave them a hundred thousand," he said. When fantasies of this caliber seize the imagination, the amount can soon rise into the millions unless someone changes the subject. In this case, someone did, by announcing that it was time to eat.

In any event, it all now seems quite academic, because none of this money, regardless of the amount, ever filtered very far down the generations. My grandfather Marion Irelan lost his farm during the Great Depression and died without a dime in his pocket. I could have used some of William and Elizabeth Jane's money. My parents could have used some in the summer of 1936.

So there's no point in wondering how much money William and Elizabeth Jane acquired. They did their best to provide for their family, but now the money is gone. All of it. And everyone knows how much zero is.

THE TANK

Uncle Clell was the youngest of my father's eleven brothers and sisters. Some people theorize that the youngest child in a large family often develops a mild, easy-going disposition. Based on my observations of Uncle Clell, I would say that his personality supported this theory. I never saw him get upset about anything. If he ever spoke a word in anger, I wasn't around to hear it.

Uncle Clell entered this life in 1911 and subsequently attended Buttontown Grade School, just as all his older brothers and sisters had done. As an adult, Uncle Clell was taller than my father, but he resembled him closely in many other ways — with dark hair, a neat mustache, a well-formed nose, a high forehead, and a love of humor. Like my father, Uncle Clell followed a course of study in normal training at Bloomfield High School, where he graduated at the age of eighteen. Unlike my father, he managed to get to Bloomfield for the qualifying exam required for teacher certification. He passed the test with ease and began teaching in the country schools of Davis County in 1929, the first year of the Great Depression. "He taught for one year at a school called Clay College," my aunt Mabel told me as we sat in the front room of her house in Ottumwa one warm September afternoon in 2001. "The next year he taught at IXL." IXL happened to be the same school where I began my education eighteen years after Uncle Clell had taught there.

As far as I know, Uncle Clell was a fine teacher. But during his year at IXL, an unhappy problem arose. "Because of the Depression," Aunt Mabel said, "the county had no money to pay him. He taught nine months without pay." In those days, the teacher often lived with the parents of the children in the school, moving from family to family as the year progressed, so perhaps Uncle Clell received room and board. How he paid for clothing and other necessities remains a mystery. I'm sure the other teachers in the system faced the same problems.

After the school year ended, the county finally managed to come up with the money to pay the teachers, including Uncle Clell. But he could see that he had entered a precarious line of work. He wanted to marry and raise a family, which you cannot do with any degree of comfort if you get paid only once a year. So he gave up schoolteaching and took a job with a prosperous farmer north of Ottumwa. But the Depression made work of this sort as precarious as schoolteaching. This year's prosperous farmer could become next year's bankrupt farmer, and the pay wasn't all that good anyway.

Uncle Clell wanted security, so he went out and found it. With the kind of boldness that my father and his brothers repeatedly displayed, Uncle Clell walked into the hiring office of the John Morrell and Company meatpacking plant in Ottumwa and announced that he wanted a job from which he would never get laid off. "He said he wanted a job that was so bad that no one else would want it," Aunt Mabel said. The man who interviewed him must have found this request for a bad job as unusual as someone asking for a broken leg. But he soon got the point and hired my uncle Clell to work in a department known as "the tank."

The men who worked in the tank processed tankage, excess fat from the hundreds of cattle and hogs slaughtered in the massive packing-house every morning, Monday through Friday. They dried the fat in huge tanks, after which someone used it to produce fertilizer or feed for livestock. When he became convinced in 1935 that he had found a secure job, Uncle Clell married Mabel Cassill, who had grown up on a farm on the north edge of Ash Grove, not far from the farm where my mother grew up. Aunt Mabel was one of my mother's dearest friends, and her marriage to my father's brother only increased that friendship.

"We didn't have much to start with," Aunt Mabel told me, "but then neither did anyone else. Clell always kept his job and we did the best we could. Lots of people had nothing at all, no jobs and no place to find one." I mentioned the year 1936. "Chinch bugs and grasshoppers," she said instantly. "We planted a garden, but they took everything." I didn't ask whether she had raised any eggplant.

Life improved after the Depression, but other problems could still arise. One day when I was fourteen, my aunt Dottla told me that Aunt Mabel had a distant cousin named R. V. Cassill who wrote dirty books. "I don't know why he has so little respect for his family," Aunt Dottla said. "The Cassills have always been very decent people, and now he's become an embarrassment to the whole family. He lives out east some-place. I hope he stays there."

I told Aunt Dottla how much I agreed with her and that I wondered how any man could do such a thing. I always quickly stated that I agreed with anything my aunts, uncles, parents, and grandparents said. I had become aware at an early age that I didn't know very much and hoped that if I paid attention to the adults I might someday know everything they did. But I always made a special point of displaying complete agreement with Aunt Dottla. My aunt Dottla was a strong-willed woman, and an argument with her would have proved about as successful as thirty seconds in the ring with Sugar Ray Robinson.

Nonetheless, at the next opportunity I rushed to the Bloomfield Public Library and checked out every book in the place by R. V. Cassill, the noted smut peddler who had disgraced his family. In the privacy of my bedroom, I began reading at a frantic pace in order to get to the good parts. But after finishing the first of these books and half of another, I had to acknowledge that my definition of "dirty book" was far different from Aunt Dottla's. R. V. Cassill's books were about as dirty as an episode of *I Love Lucy*. Adolescent males may not be as studious as their parents would like, but let me assure you of one thing: A fourteen-year-old boy knows dirt when he sees it.

Not long ago, I asked Aunt Mabel whether she remembered a cousin named R. V. Cassill who wrote novels. Although she's getting along in years, Aunt Mabel still has a perfect memory. She gave this question a moment of thought, then said, "No, I don't remember anyone who went by that name."

Poor Aunt Dottla. So much distress, and all for nothing. The failed pornographer had embarrassed no one in Aunt Mabel's family because he was in no way related to her family. And, if I may say so, he wasted the better part of a day in my fourteenth year when I should have been hoeing the garden.

———

When Aunt Mabel told me the story of Uncle Clell's search for a secure job, I could not ask Uncle Clell what was so unpleasant about the tank, for he was no longer with us. But Aunt Mabel said, "One of the worst things about it was the smell."

I know something about the smell of packinghouses, for I worked in that same plant part of the summer of my nineteenth year. I was just a kid they hired to work the vacation days of the regular workers, and the company quickly let me go when the vacation season ended. The foreman's exact words on that occasion were "You're off." I found this announcement a bit terse, but I understood that I didn't need to come back the next day.

During my brief career with John Morrell and Company, I worked in the freezers, the bacon department, the canned ham department, and in an attic where I assembled cardboard boxes and put them onto a conveyer belt that went through an opening and down to the floor below, although no one ever told me where the boxes stopped or what anyone put into them.

The best of these jobs was in the canned ham department, for when the line shut down at noon, the young and limber workers could climb a ladder to the roof and eat the food from their dinner buckets while gazing southward at the Des Moines River, or at the south side of town where at least twenty of my relatives lived in small frame houses, or at the distant bluffs that outlined the southern edge of the wide flood plain.

But the most memorable job I had that summer was in the mink-food department, which was located somewhere in a windowless cellar. The smell in that place may have come close to what Uncle Clell experienced during his years in the tank. Prepare yourself, for I am about to tell you what goes into the food that is fed to the minks that grow up to become the mink coats that some people wear. Keep in mind that a slaughterhouse throws nothing away. If it buys a one-thousand-pound steer, the company finds a use for each of those one thousand pounds.

Here is a list of what we put into the mink food, as well as I can recall it from that distant summer: tripe (cattle stomachs), various unidentifiable entrails, a bucket of blood, a light-brown powdery substance made of ingredients no one ever listed for me, cattle skulls with the hides removed but with the eyes intact and bulging outward in a disturbing fashion, and other loathsome cattle remains I can no longer remember. Because I worked during the breaks for each of the other men, I performed every job every day. Instructions were minimal. "Put in some of them tripe," one man said as he walked away my first morning in the mink-food department. My fellow workers and I threw all these delicacies into a large machine that ground them up and sent them somewhere to be canned or packaged in some fashion. I never heard anyone make a joke in the mink-food department, and I never saw anyone smile.

But I worked at the packinghouse for only part of one summer. Uncle Clell worked there forty-one years until he retired in 1973, shortly before the plant closed forever. By then he had been promoted to timekeeper in the lard refinery. If anyone thinks this is a small accomplishment, go try it. The first thirty years are the hardest.

One of my other uncles worked in the same plant at that time. I caught a glimpse of Uncle Claude one day, but I don't think he saw me. I never saw Uncle Clell at the packinghouse. The plant was so huge, consisting of at least twelve interconnected multistory buildings, that I sometimes got lost and had to ask somebody the way out at the end of the day. No one minded telling me. Everyone else had gotten lost when they first started working there.

I remember Uncle Clell clearly from the later years of his employment at the packinghouse. I never heard him complain about his duties or the conditions under which he worked. I once heard someone ask him how his job was going. "They always pay me on time," he said with a smile. He had a family of five children to support and felt lucky that he could pay the bills a family always generates. In particular, he liked having a job where he got paid more than once a year, even though a schoolhouse must have smelled a good deal better than the tank.

One time many years later, when I had young children of my own and was working for a large corporation, Uncle Clell asked me how the job was going. My job was about as much fun as a body cast, and I was about to tell him why, when I suddenly realized my selfishness. "Uncle Clell," I said, "they always pay me on time."

He laughed sincerely and patted me on the back. "Patrick," he said, "that's the kind of job to get."

My favorite photograph of Uncle Clell shows him with a baseball team sponsored by John Morrell and Company. The company used baseball teams, picnics, and other inexpensive benefits in an attempt to keep the workers happy without having to pay them what they deserved. This strategy ultimately failed when the workers organized Local No. 1 of the United Packinghouse Workers of America in 1937. Local No. 1 became one of the most militant and successful locals in the history of that union.

Uncle Clell wanted more pay like everyone else, but he also liked to play baseball. The photo of the team he played on shows ten young men and an older man who apparently served as their manager. Uncle Clell and four other men are down on one knee in the front row. The

Clell Irelan appears at the lower left in this image of one of the many baseball teams sponsored by the John Morrell and Company meatpacking plant in Ottumwa, Iowa. This picture, circa 1930s, shows the coach and team from the tank department. Photograph courtesy of Mabel Cassill Irelan.

manager and five more men are standing behind them. Seven of the players and the manager are white. Three of the players are black. All the players look healthy and full of hope for the future. Uncle Clell appears on the left end of the front row, staring intently at the camera. Except for Uncle Clell, I don't know the names of any of the other men or what happened to them. Three of the players in the front row are holding a board on which someone has painted the word TANK. Because my uncle played on this team, I assume it won every game.

———————

After Uncle Clell died at the age of eighty-nine in the year 2000, I drove down to the funeral in Ottumwa. I expressed my regrets to some of my cousins and other relatives standing near the door. Then I walked into the funeral chapel and sat down beside Aunt Mabel, where I tried to say what is impossible to say.

About five minutes later, three men I had never seen before walked in. All of them were about eighty years old, and all appeared to be in better physical condition than I. Aunt Mabel immediately introduced us, and then I remembered. In addition to his skill at baseball, Uncle Clell had been a championship bowler, and these men were his former teammates. "Clell was the best," one of them said. "Do you know what his highest game was?" I confessed that I didn't. "Two hundred and ninety-nine." I knew enough about bowling to realize that that score was one point shy of a perfect game.

"Do you know what Clell did when that last pin didn't fall?" one of the other men said.

"No," I said.

"He stood there for a second. Then he turned around and laughed."

That's how Uncle Clell did everything. He went straight at it and accepted the results. On that day, he missed perfection by one pin. Then he did what he would have done no matter what. He turned around and laughed.

THE ROCK ISLAND

In 1948, my father left the CB&Q and went to work for the Chicago, Rock Island and Pacific Railroad Company, informally known as the Rock Island Railroad, the Rock Island Lines, or simply the Rock Island. Neither my sister nor I knows why he did this, although we assume the pay was better with the Rock Island. Unfortunately, I cannot document this assumption because Pete's records for the years from 1948 to 1952 are contained in one of the small bound notebooks I can't find.

My sister recalls that one of Pete's first jobs with the Rock Island was as a towerman at the Eldon freight yard. Eldon stands on a bluff overlooking the Des Moines River about twenty miles from my parents' farm. The depot was in Eldon, but the freight yard stood on the broad flood plain across the river. A steel-truss bridge erected on huge concrete piers connected the two locations. Two lines intersected at Eldon, which explains why the railroad had built a freight yard at that spot.

In the yard, where switch engines ran endlessly back and forth along parallel lines of track, the towermen, engineers, conductors, and brakemen had the task of making sure that every freight car got detached from one train when necessary and reattached to another train bound for the right destination. From the top of the two-story tower, from where he could see the whole freight yard through broad windows, the towerman directed this entire process. If a car went to the wrong destination, a client would call and say unkind things to a manager in Chicago, and the manager would exaggerate those comments and pass them on to the crew at the yard. My father had frequently worked as a towerman for the CB&Q. He knew everything about the job. He never sent a car to the wrong destination.

At some point in 1950, as I recall from that distant year, Pete obtained the job of swing-shift operator at the Rock Island depot in Allerton, Iowa, a town of about seven hundred people sixty miles west of our farm. On the Burlington Railroad, the depot worker on any shift was called the "agent." But on the Rock Island, only the man working the first trick carried that title. This job always went to the worker with the most seniority, who also received a higher rate of pay than the others. The men who worked the second and third tricks were called "operators," an abbreviation for "telegraph operator."

Because of a long tradition, the origin of which I do not know, railroad telegraphers rarely called themselves "railroad telegraphers." They also avoided the terms "telegrapher" and "telegraph operator," except when used in official documents such as union contracts negotiated by the Order of Railroad Telegraphers. In their personal copies of those contracts, the operators gladly signed their names and listed their occupation as "telegrapher."

I have a copy of one of those contracts, all 149 pages of it, printed in 1956 and signed by my father. The first page declares that "This book is the joint property of The Order of Railroad Telegraphers and The Chicago, Rock Island and Pacific Railroad Company." The page goes on to state that the employee must return the book when requested or pay the railroad one dollar. This creates a substantial burden of guilt for me, because my father obviously did not return the book, and, if I were a betting man, I would wager a sizable amount that he never paid the Rock Island its dollar. I would happily relieve this load of guilt by paying the dollar myself, were it not for the fact that the Chicago, Rock Island & Pacific Railroad Company no longer exists.

As the swing-shift operator at Allerton, my father worked the rest days for each of the other men. On Sunday, he worked from eight in the morning until four in the afternoon, which always gave him a convenient excuse for not going to church on Sunday morning and caused me to dream of following in his footsteps. I much preferred the roar of a freight train to the organ music of Johann Sebastian Bach. On Monday and Tuesday, Pete worked from four in the afternoon until midnight. Then he had a full twenty-four hours off until midnight on Wednesday, after which he worked from midnight until eight in the morning on Thursday and Friday. Saturday was his day off. He worked this sleep-killing schedule for fifteen years, and I can personally testify that it did nothing to improve his disposition.

After he began working at Allerton, my father frequently took me to the depot with him when school wasn't in session. I don't know why he did this. I never asked. I wasn't the kind of child who asked questions. I just watched and listened. Regardless of his reasons, that tradition now provides me with the fondest memories of my childhood.

I quickly assumed a proprietary interest in the depot, the tracks and sidings adjacent to the depot, and all the freight cars parked on the sidings on any particular day. I inspected the office, the train-order hoops, and the pieces of cheap hemp string used to attach the orders to the hoops. I sat in the operator's chair in the bay window and peered up and down the track to make sure that all was ready for the next train. I observed the signal lights to ensure that they were working, although I had no idea what the various colors indicated to the engineers.

While still seated in the bay window, I inspected the telegraph keys. I also gave special attention to the sounder, which never fell silent for more than a few seconds, wondering all the while what the repeated sound of two clicks, each pair separated by a long or short interlude, could possibly mean and how my father could instantly tell which messages were of importance to him and which were not. When the sounder did announce something important to him, he rushed to the typewriter and typed furiously until the message ended.

I often read these telegrams, which the operators typed entirely in capital letters on cheap yellow paper, and I found that they made very little sense to me, owing to the fact that the agents and operators used abbreviations in the interest of saving time. One of the many useful documents that have fallen into my possession is an eighty-page booklet published in Chicago on May 1, 1944, bearing the title *Rock Island Lines: Telegraph Brevity Code*. Excluding front matter, this booklet contains seventy-six pages of abbreviations, with each page listing about twenty-five. Using the multiplication skills acquired in my one-room country school, I have calculated that the booklet contains about one thousand nine hundred abbreviations. You may be interested in knowing, for example, that EMBALM means *En route via Air Express*, that WET means *Wire quick weather conditions your territory*, and that PUD means *Pick up and delivery*. Whether any operator or agent ever learned all one thousand nine hundred of these abbreviations remains a matter of conjecture.

I recently discovered two telegrams my father saved, the first of which illustrates the use of the telegraph brevity code:

TRENTON [Missouri] 703 AM SEPT 11

RDR ALLERTON
NO 15 AND 16 WILL NOT BE HELD FOR EXPRESS UNLOADING.
WHEN THRU LOADING AND UNLOADING US MAIL THESE

TRAINS WILL BE PERMITTED TO LEAVE TOWN. ACK JOINT
HSU RDR R-11-5

MRE

At first this message carries a certain amount of meaning, even to my untrained mind. But then it disintegrates into a form of expression as mysterious as the Rosetta stone. I have no idea who Mr. MRE of Trenton was, but later that same day he grew even more truculent about the matter of loading and unloading mail on trains 15 and 16:

TRENTON 9/11

AGT
OPRS ALLERTON
WHEN WORKING MAIL ON NO 16 AND 15 AT ALLERTON DO NOT
TAKE TIME TO SORT MAIL WHILE LOADING AND UNLOADING
CAUSING DELAY TO TRAIN. MAIL CAN BE SORTED AFTER TRAIN
LEAVES TOWN AND CLERKS ON TRAIN CAN SORT OUT THEIR
SACKS AFTER LEAVING TOWN. IF YOU HAVE ANY TROUBLE
LOADING AND UNLOADING UNSORTED MAIL AND MAIL CLERKS
GIVE YOU ANY TROUBLE GET THEIR BADGE NUMBER, TRAIN
AND TIME AND ADVISE ME AT TRENTON.

MRE

In this telegram, MRE seems to have forgotten the need for brevity in what appears to have been an ongoing dispute between him and the U.S. postal clerks. But as a child, I didn't have time for these petty squabbles. I had more important work to do.

After finding the office to be in good order, I inspected the objects in the waiting room: the ticket window, the coal stove, the long wooden benches securely bolted to the floor, and a blackboard designed for the posting of passenger train schedules, but which, for want of time, no operator or agent ever used. In all honesty I must also report that I couldn't help noticing a certain lack of cleanliness and tidiness in the waiting room, although my father did occasionally scatter sweeping compound on the floor and sweep the place out.

Having inspected the waiting room, I went on to the freight room, where enormous wooden baggage carts with steel-rimmed wheels awaited the next passenger train. Here one could also find small freight orders scheduled to go out on the baggage cars of passenger trains by special arrangement with the Railway Express Agency, from which the operators collected small monthly commissions. Along with the small freight, one could also find carefully labeled gray canvas mailbags, which would go out on the mail cars of passenger trains, where the mail clerks who so displeased Mr. MRE would sort the mail while holstered .38-caliber revolvers dangled from their belts in case the murderous James brothers, Frank and Jesse, should rise from their graves and go in search of another train to rob.

I would have moved on at that point to an inspection of the room where the section men stored their tools and equipment, but they wisely kept that room secured with a large padlock so that little boys could not go in, stumble about in the darkness, and emerge with their heads bruised and lacerated. So I went outside instead to inspect the condition of the double line of tracks and also the sidings. I checked the tracks themselves, the steel plates and bolts that connected them to each other, the creosote-soaked ties, the steel spikes that secured the tracks to the ties, and the ballast between the ties that held the entire track in place.

Finally, in direct violation of all Rock Island rules and regulations, I climbed the ladders of the boxcars to make sure the steel roofs had not blown away. Thus reassured, I returned to the depot platform to conduct my most important duty of all: the inspection of every train that passed through the village of Allerton while my father was on duty.

By this era, the Rock Island had replaced all of its steam locomotives with diesel engines, so I missed seeing the line's giant coal-burning locomotives with all their power, precision, and excitement. But since I didn't know what I had missed, I was quite content with the railroad's dark-red streamlined diesels, with the line's distinctive red, white, and black logo on the nose of the engine.

Ten passenger trains a day passed through little Allerton, five eastbound and five westbound, although two of those eastbound trains soon turned north on the Short Line and ended their run at Minneapolis and St. Paul. The freight trains passed by so often that I never even tried to count them. Included among the passenger trains was the Rock Island's luxury express from Chicago to Los Angeles, the *Golden State Limited*, although railroad workers never used the name of any train except when dealing with the public. Among themselves, they spoke only a train's number. Thus, they referred to the *Golden State* merely as train No. 3 when westbound and train No. 4 when eastbound. In fact, all westbound trains carried odd numbers, and all eastbound trains had even numbers. The name *Golden State* by itself failed to tell the railroad employees something they desperately needed to know: the direction in which the train was going.

Boarding a train at a small town like Allerton was entirely different from boarding a train at a terminal such as La Salle Street Station in Chicago. When you arrived at La Salle Street Station, the train was waiting for you. When you arrived at a small-town depot like Allerton's, you waited for the train. The waiting, anticipation, and growing excitement made the difference. To this you could add the gradual transformation of the depot from a lonely little building into a place of intense interest, activity, and urgency. When you first saw the light of the locomotive in the distance and heard the sound of the whistle, you could not repress the feeling of elation that caused your pulse to quicken and your body to tremble.

The train approached the depot with a great display of its power and importance: a whistle in response to my father's signal with flag or lantern, a long blast for the grade crossings east and west of the depot, clouds of steam from the locomotive and the dining car, a final squeal as the air brakes gripped and held, bringing the train to a dead stop exactly where the conductor wanted it.

Just before the train stopped, the porter hopped off. Like all railroad men, he made every move with the grace of an entertainer, placing the Pullman stool exactly where he knew the steps of the coach would come to a halt. The next man to step onto the platform had an obsession with only one thing: Time. The polished metal letters on the front of his blue cap spelled "Conductor." He was in charge of that train, and the one thing he wanted most in all the world was to get it moving again. Conductors could not bear the sight of a motionless train.

The conductor had the assistance at every moment of the passenger train brakeman, whose overwhelming ambition in life was to become a conductor. Thus, during those few frustrating minutes in which the train stood still at the depot, these two men became intensely engaged in two activities: alternately looking at their pocket watches and overseeing the movement of passengers, baggage, small freight, and mailbags — none of which would ever move at a speed acceptable to them. These were the frustrations of men forced to work in a world governed by the agonizing physical laws of time and space, and by the physical and psychological limitations of human beings.

Finally, when everything had found its place, the brakeman climbed aboard, the porter followed with the Pullman stool, the conductor took a final glance at his watch before signaling the engineer with the broad overhand sweep of the highball, the engineer responded with a brief blast from the whistle, the train started to move, and the conductor stepped aboard and turned around to wave farewell to my father, a broad smile now consuming his face for the first time. Leaning for a moment against a baggage cart, Pete raised a triumphant wave in response, while in the departing locomotive, the engineer pulled back on the throttle so slowly and smoothly that when he had finally reached a cruising speed of eighty miles an hour, not a single drop of wine had soiled the tablecloths in the dining car.

At that moment, far to the rear, the depot had again become part of a small, lonely town, where everyone and everything moved slowly, calmly, and quietly, and where a little boy had curled up in one of the office chairs for a brief nap before the arrival of the next train.

━━━━━━

Like the porters and all other railroad men, my father was a showman. This quality revealed itself most in his handling of train orders. A train order was nothing more than a quickly typed message, usually in duplicate, giving instructions to the engineer and conductor of a freight train about any number of matters, such as where to pick up or drop off a boxcar, where to stop at an elevator to take on one or more carloads of grain, where and when to stop and wait for another freight train in order to exchange a boxcar, where to slow down for sections of track under repair, or when to drop off a car or locomotive at the line's mammoth repair shops in Silvis, Illinois. Sometimes the orders for the engineer and conductor would differ slightly, depending on their individual tasks and what awaited them down the line.

The operators also prepared train orders for passenger trains. These concerned matters such as track conditions at specific spots, slow orders for sections of track in need of repair, delays to expect because of other trains running behind schedule, and many other matters I never managed to learn. In spite of my childhood timidity, I sometimes tried to ask my father a question, but he rarely had time to answer. Like all operators and agents on the Rock Island, he did the work of two men every day. The managers in Chicago thought this was good business practice.

Radios now transmit train orders, but when Pete was an operator, the dispatcher in Des Moines or other operators sent each train order by telegram; and the operator at the appropriate depot typed it in duplicate, attached both copies to train-order hoops, and handed the order up to the engineer and conductor as the train sped by. If the train normally stopped at that station, the operator used a train-order hoop for the engineer and then simply handed the order to the conductor on the depot platform.

The first train-order hoops consisted of long pieces of bamboo with one end bent all the way around and attached by wire to form a hoop through which the trainman would place his outstretched arm. After detaching the message from a clip, the trainman threw the hoop back off the train. This was not entirely efficient, since the operator then had to walk down the track to retrieve the hoops.

By the time Pete became an operator, train-order hoops had evolved into Y-shaped contrivances made from three sticks of wood and fastened together with a piece of metal. The operator tied the ends of a piece of string together with two slipknots, inserted the train order between the knots, and pulled them securely together. Next he attached the string to the triangle-shaped part of the hoop at the top of the Y by means of grooves at the ends of the two upper sticks and a metal clip at the point where all three sticks came together. The stick at the bottom was longer than the other two, forming a handle for the operator or agent. Then, as the train roared past, the operator held up the hoop and the engineer's outstretched arm pulled off the piece of string with the attached train order, leaving the hoop in the operator's hand. Finally, using another hoop already prepared in the same manner, the operator followed the same procedure with the conductor on the rear platform of the caboose. In the case of a passenger train, the conductor stood at the door of one of the coaches.

All this sounds quite simple, but as with so many simple matters, things could easily go wrong. Consider the case of a freight train. First of all, if the train didn't have a stop scheduled at the operator's station, it could be traveling as fast as seventy or eighty miles an hour. Second, the operator got only one chance with the train order for the engineer and one chance with the copy for the conductor. Third, both the engineer and the conductor had to successfully pull the string with the attached train order from the hoop. If one got the order and the other didn't, this did them little good at all, because the engineer and the conductor were at the opposite ends of a long freight train and had no way of talking to each other. Finally, if the trainmen did not get the train order, the engineer had to stop the train. This was not a simple matter. Depending on how many cars the engine was pulling and how fast the train was going, it could take the engineer a mile or more to bring it to a stop. Then it had to back up.

As a general rule, engineers didn't like to back up. They were in the business of getting from point A to point B as fast as possible. Backing up involved leaving point A and returning to point A, which ran counter to everything they knew about the operation of railroad locomotives. So an event such as this would, without question, cause the operator a great deal of embarrassment. It would delay that train, which would cause delays for other trains as well, and all trainmen hated delays.

I watched my father hand up train orders for fifteen years. He never missed. His movements were as precise as Arturo Toscanini's. Using a long hoop for the engineer and a shorter one for the conductor, he placed himself on the platform at track side, legs spread about two feet apart, suit jacket buttoned, one hand grasping the stick, the entire hoop held parallel to the platform. He waited for the engineer to lean out the window and place his arm in a precise position, from which it would not move. With everything in place, Pete waited until the last instant, then swung the hoop up to the exact height required. He didn't have to wait that long to raise the hoop. He didn't have to make it look so dramatic. He was performing, entertaining the audience at the Rock Island Theater in Allerton that day.

The engineers loved him. They grinned like children as they flew past with the whistle frozen in a deafening blare for the grade crossings. They kept waiting for him to miss, but he wouldn't do it. He refused to miss. If he ever had, they would have been elated. It would not have angered them. It would not have made them cross. It would have come as a surprise ending to a long performance, but Pete didn't approve of surprise endings.

———

Not long ago, I stopped at a place in Illinois where the public can sit and watch the trains go by. Simultaneously, loudspeakers allow you to listen to the dispatcher talking to the trainmen on the radio and the trainmen talking among themselves. The spot stood at a safe, well-chosen location, and everyone was polite and friendly. But somehow it didn't seem quite right. Something was missing. The thrill was missing. I wanted to see the theater curtain open one more time, to sense the power of the oncoming train, to hear the scream of the whistle, to see the engineer's outstretched arm, to feel my body tremble with anticipation, and finally to watch a black-haired man in a blue suit and silk tie enact one more perfect performance.

CENTRAL STANDARD

During World War II, the federal government imposed year-round daylight savings time on the entire nation as a means of diverting fuel consumption from civilian to military use. By setting the clocks ahead one hour, the sun appeared to set an hour later than before, and people turned on their electric lights an hour later, thereby allowing the power companies to use less fuel for the production of electricity. The energy saved could then be used to manufacture armaments. After the war ended, the central government returned control of the country's clocks to state and local governments, most of which went back to standard time. I should point out that many authorities in the history of time keeping insist that the correct term is daylight *saving* time, not daylight *savings* time, but because the remaining two hundred and fifty million people in the country say daylight "savings" time, I will meekly follow the practice of the multitude.

During the war, many people, especially city people, had found that they liked daylight savings time, especially in the summer, because it permitted them to spend more time in their backyards in the evenings, doing whatever it was that people did in their backyards in those days. Since the country was becoming more urban every year, the opinions of these people grew increasingly important. Nonetheless, many people and institutions still opposed daylight savings time, including farmers and railroads. Because my father was both a farmer and a railroad man, it will come as no surprise that he opposed daylight savings time.

The debate over this issue continued throughout the fifties and into the sixties. In Iowa, one member of the state legislature made himself the darling of newspaper columnists across the country by proclaiming during an official legislative session that standard time was "God's time." Comedians, news writers, and anyone else who cared to join in the fun made great sport of the notion that the Almighty was using his infinite power tinkering with the clocks in Des Moines.

My father preferred to keep his discussion of this issue entirely secular and made no attempt to summon divine powers to his side. I recall one occasion when he explained to an in-law, a cheerful, rotund man from Philadelphia, how daylight savings time complicated a farmer's life. "If you feed your calves their corn at seven o'clock in the morning all summer long, that's the time they'll always come in from the pasture and line up at the feedbunk. But if you suddenly set your clock back an hour in the fall, the cattle still expect to be fed at the same time as before, even though your clock now says it's only six o'clock instead of seven."

"So why not let them wait?" the man said in his metropolitan innocence.

"Spend the night with us this fall and you'll see why not," Pete said, leaning back in his chair the way people do when they're positive of something. "If you don't feed them when they expect it, they'll start to bellow. Do you have any idea how much noise twenty Angus steers can make when they all start bellowing at the same time?" He tilted his head to the side and waited.

"No, I don't. You'd better tell me."

"Enough noise to wake the dead. Enough to wake a whole graveyard. They'll make so much noise they'll get you out of bed and into the barnyard in your pajamas. And it won't do any good to hang a clock on the barn. Cows' clocks are in their stomachs, and as I'm sure you know, a cow has four stomachs."

The in-law from Philadelphia made no response to that comment. He was a psychology major and probably hadn't made a detailed study of livestock stomachs. "So what do you do if the state goes on fast time?" he said, returning to the original subject.

"You ignore it. You don't change your clocks. You don't change your watch. You stay on standard time all year long."

And that is precisely what a great many farmers did when their states adopted daylight savings time. I'm sure many beef and dairy farmers still do the same thing today. The Rock Island and many other railroads also refused to change. The words "Central Standard Time" began to appear at the top of every timetable for every passenger train in the central time zone all year long. To have reprinted timetables and rescheduled connecting trains twice each year would have created an additional expense that the Rock Island could not afford, for by then that railroad had begun the long, slow decline that would lead to its extinction in 1980. When the federal government imposed daylight savings time on the entire country in 1966, the railroads had to capitulate, but they didn't like it.

In February of 1965, Pete secured the agent's job at the Rock Island depot in Keosauqua, a beautiful little town on the Big Bend of the Des Moines River, about thirty miles east of my parent's farm. Keosauqua was the same town where my father had worked for the WPA during the dreadful summer of 1936 — the summer of grasshoppers, dust storms, and eggplant. Things were better in 1965.

But not for long.

What my father did not know in February of 1965 was that the Rock Island had already decided to close the depot at Keosauqua, which it proceeded to do in January of 1966. Pete had plenty of seniority by then, so the railroad offered him a job somewhere out west. But my father had already worked in the West more than thirty years before — first with Western Union, then with the CB&Q — and he said what he often said when pushed too far: "I've had a bellyful of it." He and my mother had paid off the indebtedness on their house and farm, most of their relatives lived nearby, Pete was fifty-nine years old, and my mother was happy in her church and community. My father said he wouldn't go. The railroad replied that he had to take that job or no job.

But the Order of Railroad Telegraphers took an altogether different view of the matter. The union had adopted a new name in 1965, but I share my father's superstition that it's bad luck to change the name of anything, so I'll continue to use the old name. The Order of Railroad Telegraphers said, "Give the man a decent amount of severance pay or we'll see you in court." After lengthy negotiations, the Rock Island finally awarded Pete $7,893.50 in severance pay, minus $1,105.09 for taxes and $32.06 for the federal government's Railroad Retirement System, the precursor and model for the Social Security System. That was his reward from the Chicago, Rock Island & Pacific Railroad Company after eighteen years of service. It averages out to $438.53 per year. The railroad did not provide a pension for any of its workers except the managers.

My father's last day of work for the Rock Island Railroad fell on January 15, 1966, almost thirty years after leaving for Lincoln, Nebraska, to become a depot agent for the CB&Q. On his last day at the depot in

Keosauqua, he earned $21.92, $2.74 an hour. Don't go in search of that depot. The company tore it down and ripped up the rails.

But my father always remained a railroad man. It's something you can't retire from. He never owned a wristwatch. He carried his Hamilton Railway Special for the rest of his life. And I'm sure he never defiled it with daylight savings time.

———

In August of 2001, I traveled with my daughter Claire from Mount Pleasant, Iowa, to Chicago via Amtrak train No. 6, the *California Zephyr*, and returned by the same route two days later on train No. 5. In 1941, while still employed by the CB&Q, my father had worked almost the entire year in the same depot where Claire and I patiently waited for our train. The brick building and platform appeared to be in fine repair, as did the depot's interior, with its white-tile wainscoting, its long oak benches divided into individual seats by large armrests, and its brass bars at the ticket window.

The agent handed us our tickets and advised us that No. 6 was running late because of track repairs under way near Ottumwa. I told him that we were on vacation, that we were not in a hurry, and that we would rather spend eternity in a depot than five minutes in an airport. The agent liked the sound of this overstatement, and we began exchanging stories.

The sandy-haired agent with a neat mustache told me about all the depots he had worked in. I expressed my admiration for his career and tried not to show how envious I felt. I then launched into the story of the night when Curtis Adcock, my mother's cousin, had clung to the throttle of his Chicago, Milwaukee & St. Paul steam locomotive as it leapt from the tracks just short of the bridge and hurtled into the Des Moines River in Ottumwa. The locomotive and tender sank, but Adcock and the fireman did not and soon found themselves back at work in a new locomotive, despite allegations by certain liars and thieves that my mother's cousin was a notorious highballer whose recklessness had caused the plunge.

The agent, a man about fifteen years younger than I, showed sincere interest in this account, so I went on to the night when another of my mother's cousins, George Santee — a freight conductor for the Gulf, Mobile & Ohio — had slipped on the ice-covered ladder of a boxcar and fallen onto the track, where the next car severed both of his legs just above the knees. I don't know what happened to George Santee after that, but I do know that his father, Zebulon Santee, had worked as a fireman and engineer for the Milwaukee Road and that the company had found less demanding jobs for him when his health began to fail, ultimately putting him in charge of the water tank in the coal-mining town of Mystic, Iowa. I could only hope that the Gulf, Mobile & Ohio had treated George as well as the Milwaukee had treated his father.

At this point, knowing that the agent had work to do, I left him in peace. Forty-five minutes later, he announced that No. 6 would arrive in four minutes. The waiting room emptied, and the train reached Mount Pleasant about an hour behind schedule. The conductor's crew hit the ground and began communicating by means of hand-held radios with the engineer, who adroitly maneuvered the train to accommodate passengers, luggage, small freight, and mail. Several passengers stepped from the coaches and greeted their waiting families. All members of the conductor's crew wore dark-blue pants and white shirts. None wore identifying caps, so I asked the woman who took our tickets if she was the conductor. She smiled and said, "No, but I'm the conductor's assistant." The expression on her face, the rhythm of her movements, and the tenor of her voice told me everything else I needed to know. The railroad was in her blood, and nothing could ever replace it.

In less than five minutes, No. 6 pulled away from the depot. The track east of Mount Pleasant gave no indication of needing repairs, and the man at the throttle soon had us cruising at seventy-five to eighty miles an hour. Children slept beside their mothers. The welded rails yielded no sound. The ride was as smooth as apricot brandy. Claire sat beside me, making the trip I had often promised but never delivered until that day. Beyond the window, I saw the gentle rise and fall of the land I will never leave.

At that moment, in my childlike innocence, everything seemed perfect — everything but the voice across the aisle, which began to complain loudly and ceaselessly about the lateness of the train. I tried to ignore this noise, but finally turned to see what it came from. Its source originated from a young woman sitting beside her mother. Her skin had a gray hue, and her hair was a sickly yellow. The dress she wore fit her with less charm than a feed sack. She seemed to be suffering from the delusion that Amtrak owned the tracks that had caused the delay, when in fact the Burlington Northern Santa Fe Railroad owned the tracks and strove to keep them in the best condition possible at all times.

I longed at that moment for the presence of my mother, who would have listened to these insults to her old CB&Q for a very short time before turning to the young woman and telling her that she should be thankful that the men were working on the tracks in order to make them safe for all passengers and trainmen on the line, and that the woman should stop complaining and try to find something useful to do.

But my mother was not with us and never would be again, and I lacked her strength, fearlessness, and fiery temper and could not bring myself to deliver the needed rebuke. I did consider asking the conductor whether he could toss the woman off the train at Burlington, preferably while crossing the bridge over the Mississippi River. But I doubted that he would grant my request and that he might instead toss me into a waiting police car, which would haul me off to the nearest hospital, where a psychiatrist would ask me if I frequently entertained the notion of throwing young women off of railroad bridges.

Finally, the woman's own mother grew sick of her daughter's whining and told her forcefully to "chill." This command had the desired effect, I added the word "chill" to my working vocabulary, and we rode the remaining miles to Chicago and into the train shed at Union Station in relative harmony between woman and machine. As Claire and I walked along the platform toward the station, I stopped to shake hands with the assistant conductor. "You'll be a conductor within six months," I said. I believe that this statement led to the first instance in my life when I could honestly say that I had seen someone "beam." The woman loved the train and so did I, and I like to think that with those words of farewell I had made her even happier than she already was.

The next day, after a restful night in an ugly new hotel on South Michigan Avenue, I subjected Claire to a number of irritants, including a hot ride on the Ravenswood El Line and a short walk to Lincoln Park, where I took an inordinate number of photographs of the Lincoln and Grant monuments. Then, because I was already in the mood and still had the instrument in my hands, I took an inordinate number of photographs of Claire.

After I had satisfied my photo-taking compulsion for the moment, Claire and I walked out of the park and headed south on Lake Shore Drive, past the homes of the impossibly rich, past the Drake Hotel, and on down Michigan Avenue. At this point, Claire's energy began rising to levels that could not be ignored or restrained. By contrast, my energy began to diminish at an alarming rate, and my feet began to swell like inner tubes. Somewhere near the old Chicago Water Tower, with my vital signs dropping on every screen, Claire spotted a tall building that she instinctively knew contained a Bloomingdales sinkhole. Even if I had tried, I could not have resisted a fourteen-year-old daughter who was stronger, smarter, and more decisive than I.

She dragged me in, and I collapsed on an escalator that bore me ever upward to a place where I gladly signed away a mere sixty-eight dollars for a sweater bearing the letters NDKY or some variation thereof. While waiting for Claire to make her selection, I requested the use of a water fountain and a chair. The saleswoman showed me to a drinking fountain but said that she had no chairs. I looked in every direction and even sought out potential hiding places until I had to acknowledge that Bloomingdales had not yet discovered the existence of chairs. Claire finally found the right sweater, and we made our escape.

Following a ride south on the Howard Street subway, we emerged on East Monroe and walked to the Chicago Art Institute, where I had hoped to photograph the Lincoln Monument in Grant Park. But I had not anticipated the twelve-foot-high hurricane fence south of the Art Institute, behind which large men with large machines were making a holy mess of the entire bean field. Footsore and exhausted, we abandoned our original plan and returned to the hotel, which grew more ugly at every glance.

I immediately fell comatose on the bed next to the window and regained consciousness three hours later. Claire watched television during this interlude and claimed upon my recovery that I had snored loudly the whole while. I denied this unfilial charge, refused to continue the debate I was bound to lose, and invited Claire to accompany me to what might yet remain of La Salle Street Station, the former terminal of the once-mighty Chicago, Rock Island & Pacific Railroad.

She declined the invitation, but I felt no resentment, for Claire is the girl with her grandfather Pete's perfect forehead, nose, eyes, teeth, skin, and black hair. She never saw her grandfather, a man short of stature like his ancient Celtic ancestors on those two green islands off the west coast of Europe. She had never seen him signal the highball, then stand in the face of the onrushing *Golden State Limited* and casually hand up the orders as the train roared past at ninety miles an hour when the Rock Island track and roadbed were still in perfect condition and everyone believed that the best was yet to come. She had not lived in his world as I had for that brief moment called youth. And even my world, such as it was, receded at an ever-increasing pace, but Claire would be waiting for me when I returned from La Salle Street, and we would go to dinner at the Conrad Hilton, where a man named Rudolfo would treat us with what seemed like genuine kindness and where neither of us would find anything wrong with the food.

So I set off alone, camera in hand, in search of what my map of Chicago still called the "La Salle Street Station." I hoped for the best, but the station I saw and photographed late that Friday afternoon was the La Salle Street Station in name only. The old terminal of my childhood had vanished forever. Four ticket windows, a snack bar, and ten or fifteen yellow plastic chairs stood in a small waiting room. A brass plaque partially hidden behind an advertising stand said something about the heroes who had raised this new edifice. The clock on the wall was set on daylight savings time.

The station I saw as I fired away with my Japanese camera now served only commuters. I could not remember with any certainty that it even stood where the old terminal had when I was a boy many decades before. When I walked outside, I found the platforms and overhead shelters clean, functional, and attractive. Chicago's double-deck Metra trains came and left with swift efficiency as home-bound workers fled the Chicago Board of Trade and the rest of the La Salle Street financial district. Anyone with the gift of sight, sound, or humanity could sense the relief and momentary happiness that those men and women felt as they hurried through the station, down the platforms, and onto their trains. Most were younger than I. Many were not even half my age. And as they passed through the waiting room, a dim reminder of the old La Salle Street Station, the former showpiece of one of the largest and most famous railroads in the history of the United States, I wondered how many of those tired commuters knew what had once stood on that street and how much they had lost.

JANE

I have a clear recollection of my morals and behavior for my entire life. I was an angelic boy until I reached adulthood, at which time I became a model citizen and have remained one ever since. My sister, Jane, has a different recollection of her little brother.

Jane entered this life seven years before I did. Because of our difference in age, I thought when quite young that our family contained three adults and only one child. I once asked my mother if I had been an accident. Visibly amused, she said that I had been planned in every way and not to worry about it.

My sister's main challenge to my fond memory of myself as a child is that I was "spoiled rotten," perhaps the result of my broken leg at the age of three, which resulted in a great deal of sympathy from my parents, grandparents, aunts, uncles, and all other right-minded adults who knew me. Who could find fault with an angelic little boy whose leg refused to heal properly?

In all honesty, I do recall a few instances long after the broken leg when I would tease my sister to the point of distraction. She tolerated each instance of this for a reasonable period of time, after which she tried to stop me with threats of violence. When that failed, she tried or succeeded in striking me with her fists. These blows usually caused little harm, because they hit me with only glancing force, given the fact that by then I was running away as fast as I have ever run before or since.

My usual escape route took me out of the house, across the yard, and around the pond bank. My sister feared snakes, and the pond gave every appearance of containing all the snakes my favorite saint had previously driven out of Ireland. I feared snakes, too, but I feared my sister more. Unless she was really furious, she gave up the chase when I reached the pond bank, and our Lord spared my life until my next indiscretion.

For some reason, I can't remember what sorts of things I did to annoy my sister, but I remember her reactions quite vividly. "You little snot," she said, launching herself from the starting blocks quicker than Jesse Owens and aiming blows at my retreating form.

When she scored a good hit, my mother said, "Jane, if you don't stop that, you're going to kill him."

"It won't kill him," Jane said. "He's too dumb to kill." I lacked the medical knowledge to reach a firm conclusion about the likelihood of my death by fratricide, but even the fear of this did not prevent future provocations and escapes to the pond bank.

In all truthfulness, I must now reveal to the tremulous reader that my sister also exhibited profound wickedness on rare occasions, although it took a more cerebral form than my own. I recall a day on which my sister and mother were discussing something in the kitchen while I entertained myself in what rural people called the "front room." City people called this room the "living room," a term that, in my bucolic ignorance, has always mystified me. While I was engaged with my electric train, I suddenly heard my mother raise her voice and say, "Do you mean that you don't believe in the virgin birth of Christ?"

Jane said, "All I mean is that I'm not sure. I'm not saying it's not true, and I'm not saying it is true."

"Jane, if you're a Christian, this is one of the things you have to believe. Please tell me that you don't reject your faith."

"I just have some doubts," Jane said. "You don't want me to lie, do you?"

"No, Dear," Mother said. "I don't want you to lie."

I could tell that this matter was of some importance to the two adults in the kitchen, although I didn't really understand why, largely because I didn't know what the words "virgin birth" meant. Actually, I did know what "birth" meant. I lived on a farm where domestic animals gave birth to more domestic animals every spring. They did this in broad daylight without a hint of embarrassment, and no one thought this the least bit unusual. Birth seemed no more mysterious than a dish of mashed potatoes. To come to the point, it was the word "virgin" that confused me. My parents owned numerous Angus cattle, one or two Jersey milk cows, and an occasional Hereford, but no one ever said our cows were virgins.

I learned two things from the conversation between my mother and sister that day. I learned that adults worried a great deal about issues that children did not even recognize as issues, and I also learned that I must never say anything to upset my mother. I saw that if I ever came to believe in stealing, robbery, murder, or shooting out streetlights with a BB gun, I must never tell my mother of these beliefs. Beliefs seemed as important to adults as actions. I never came to believe in stealing, robbery, or murder, but I did, at the age of nine, shoot out a streetlight with a BB gun one night in Ottumwa, Iowa, and as I write these words I pray that the statute of limitations for crimes against streetlights has elapsed. I have since attributed this criminal behavior to peer pressure, although I didn't think of this excuse until I was thirty-five years old. The boy who owned the BB gun expressed his admiration for my marksmanship, but I never told my mother. I have since learned the meaning of the words "virgin birth," but I have not decided whether destruction of public property is more or less sinful than what you believe about events that allegedly occurred two thousand years ago in a place I have never seen and never will.

Eventually, I outgrew my desire to irritate my sister, and a rapprochement set in that has never ended. Whenever my parents had to leave home for a short time, they left me in the care of my sister. On those occasions, she became admirably concerned with my welfare. I recall one evening, for example, when she prepared supper for us. The meal consisted entirely of fried onion rings. I thoroughly enjoyed this supper, although I wouldn't recommend it to anyone who suffers from chronic dyspepsia.

My sister eventually entered high school, and at some point my parents decided that she was old enough to go out on dates. She had many admirers, perhaps because she had inherited my mother's nose and chin and my father's perfect blue eyes. Her blond-brown hair, cut and permed according to the fashion of the day, completed the vision that sent many a high-school boy in search of her phone number. For reasons I have never deduced, Jane would sometimes take me along on her dates, especially if a movie at the Iowa Theater in Bloomfield figured into the night's entertainment. I would sit there and absorb the meaningless words and images of the movie until life-threatening boredom set in, at which time I would go in search of my young friends.

If I found any of these friends, we proceeded to annoy the other theatergoers by making vulgar noises and throwing popcorn at the screen. This behavior inevitably attracted the attention of the manager, who told us to knock it off or he would call our parents. This was not an empty threat. The manager knew us, our parents, and almost everyone else who lived in or near Bloomfield. Life was like that in a small town. We knocked it off. But it would happen again on other nights.

Jane herself entered show business while in high school, starring in a play that I believe was called *Seventeenth Summer*. I have no idea who wrote the play and do not plan to spend any of my diminishing energy in finding out. I went to the play with my parents. I didn't understand a thing about it and remember nothing that occurred except for the conclusion. The play ended with my sister delivering a long soliloquy. I couldn't comprehend anything she said. It was something about being seventeen and being in love. I cared nothing for seventeen or love, but it amazed me that my big sister could stand there alone in the spotlight in a beautiful dress and remember all those words, which seemed to go on for about six hours.

I would like to see Jane in that play again. I think I could understand most of it now. I'm well past seventeen and am beginning to understand things I thought I never would. But Jane lives in a city far away, and I've heard nothing about a revival of *Seventeenth Summer* with the original cast at Bloomfield High School.

I'm fortunate to have had such an intelligent sister. I know that I will never be as smart as she is, but no one seems to care, least of all me. I still live in Iowa and cannot imagine living anywhere else, so if there is ever any family business to conduct, I look into it. Then I call my sister and ask her what to do. After discussing the matter, she always concludes by telling me to make the decision and she'll agree with anything I choose. "You don't even need to call me," she says. "Just go ahead and do it."

"All right," I say with cheerful confidence. I look into the matter some more and make a list of all the options. Then I call Jane again and read her the list. "What do you think we should do?" I ask. While talking about the issue and telling me again to do whatever I wish, she says which option she likes best, and that's the one I choose.

Life is less confusing if you have an older sister.

ANTIQUES

After my father left the faltering Rock Island Railroad in 1966, he did what all Americans do when faced with time on their hands: He began looking for ways to make money. He continued to raise beef cattle, but his expenses sometimes devoured his income. He drove a school bus and worked at the sale barn, but these part-time jobs yielded only modest wages. Finally, he seized upon a business perfectly suited to his skills and temperament: antique trading.

His principal business strategy had come down to him from centuries of peasant ancestors: Buy what the seller regards as trash; sell what the buyer regards as treasure. With this concept in mind, he began driving his used van through the countryside in southern Iowa and northern Missouri, looking for people who could not see the potential wealth in all the old objects they had lying about. He attended yard sales, farm sales, and estate sales. The word "used" on a business sign always set him looking for a parking space. It didn't matter what the object was. If he could buy it cheaply enough, someone else, he believed, would eventually pay him more.

I had grown up and moved away from our eighty-acre farm by then, but my visits home revealed his progress. The little one-story frame house began to fill with remarkable objects: glass balls from lightning rods, glass and ceramic insulators from telephone and telegraph poles, candlesticks of every shape and color, advertising signs for forgotten products, assorted pieces of furniture in assorted stages of disrepair, piles of turquoise jewelry purportedly made by skilled Indian craftsmen of the Southwest, and, more than anything else, fruit jars. Hundreds and hundreds of fruit jars.

"Father," I said as I looked around, "what are you ever going to do with all this junk?"

"What I'm going to do, Patrick," he said patiently, "is make money." As he said this, you could actually see his blue eyes glow.

"How?"

"Country people don't know this, but people who live in town will pay big money for antiques." My father was himself a country person, as was I, but this didn't matter. He knew something the others didn't, and now I had also learned the secret.

Thus began my father's transfer of antiques from farm to city. On every weekend that presented the opportunity, he and my mother loaded the van with old objects, especially fruit jars, and set off for Iowa City or Davenport or Chicago, where Pete had previously deposited thirty or forty dollars to reserve a table at an antique show. High school gymnasiums and lodge halls provided typical venues for these modern reenactments of the ancient impulse to acquire and discard.

Still handsome in late middle age, with a striking olive complexion and black hair flecked with gray, my father had altered his manner of dress for these antique shows. Instead of the dark suits and silk ties he had worn as a railroad telegrapher, he now adopted plaid shirts and cotton trousers to project a rural image.

My mother, once the stylish flapper but now grown matronly, still dressed as fashionably as her budget would allow. She favored traditional dresses, conservative in color and design. If she ever wore a pantsuit, I have managed to repress all recollection of it. Fortunately, she never felt the need to give her gray hair a blue tint.

Thus prepared, my parents set off for the show, Father in hopes of making money, Mother content with any excuse for an outing. Sometimes I joined them. Uncle Clell and Aunt Mabel had also gone into the antique business and often appeared at the same shows, turning those events into family reunions. I have to report that I found more interest in the reunions than in the antiques.

After my parents had carefully unwrapped each object and placed all of them on the table to draw attention to the most valuable pieces, they would sit down on the folding chairs provided by the management and wait for the urban masses to appear. And appear they did. Lots of old people, numerous middle-aged people, and many bored children.

As they passed the table, the old people could be heard saying, "I used to have one of those. Should've kept it." The middle-aged people might say, "I'd like to have one of those. How much is it?" The answer was seldom the one they wanted to hear. The children didn't say much of anything. They just whined and tugged at their parents.

To my father's dismay, it soon became apparent that his potential customers did not share his love of antique fruit jars. Their lack of interest mystified him. He had acquired so many jars and had learned so much about them. He knew the ambers, the cobalt blues, the Masons, the Presto Supreme Masons, and the Atlas Strong Shoulder Masons. He knew where they had been made, when they had been made, and how they had been made. Most important, having reviewed all the standard reference books, he knew how much, in an ideal world, each jar was worth.

The problem was that in the real world few people were willing to pay that ideal price. In fact, shortly after he had acquired a huge inventory of fruit jars, the market for them went straight into the cellar. In an event reminiscent of the legendary Dutch mania of long ago, antique fruit jars suddenly became as worthless as tulip bulbs in seventeenth-century Amsterdam.

Undeterred, my father merely stored his jars in the basement to await the inevitable market rebound. "They'll come back, Patrick," he said.

"When?" I asked.

"Someday. It's all a matter of timing."

Timing. That was the answer. In the interim, he began to specialize in antique furniture. The thing about furniture, he soon learned, is that people always need it, whether it's old or new. My father would buy a nice old piece, spend an inordinate amount of time stripping and refinishing it, and cart it off to an antique show, where something amazing would happen: Someone would buy it, and at his price. He began to make money. It wasn't a fortune, but according to the mentality inherited from his distant forebears, any reasonable profit constituted a great victory, if not an outright sign of God's favor.

But he also knew better than to announce his success publicly. To do so would be both rude and unlucky. "I took a terrible beating on that chest of drawers," he would say to the trader at the next table. "I can't make a dime at this business." Privately, he would tell Mother, Aunt Mabel, Uncle Clell, my sister, or me what he had made on a piece. And he never forgot what he had paid for something or how much he had sold it for, no matter how many years had passed. He didn't bother to write any of this down. He simply remembered it. He displayed the same memory with all the livestock he bought and sold. I wish I had inherited a little more of his memory, for I often forget the names of people I've known for twenty years.

Aunt Mabel recently pointed out to me that when Mother attended these antique shows, my father's sales increased. "Gerata was so friendly and outgoing," she said, "that people would stop to talk and end up buying something." Out of modesty, my mother never would have made this claim. I don't know what my father thought and would not have felt it polite to ask.

Eventually, Pete sold every piece of furniture he ever bought. In fact, he sold almost everything else, except for the fruit jars and the things he gave away. All that nephews, nieces, or grandchildren had to say was that they liked a certain candlestick, and he would set it aside as a future gift. Even now, as I occasionally sort through what little remains, I still come across objects marked with "Jill" or "Sara" or "Lisa" or someone else — objects perhaps forgotten by those named. My sister and I, always eager to rid ourselves of anything we can, make sure those objects find their way into the right hands.

Nonetheless, decades after the last chest of drawers went out the door, most of the fruit jars still remained in the basement. For years, my sister and I have repeatedly asked each other — first in person, then by long distance, and finally via e-mail — "What are we going to do with all the fruit jars?" Neither of us has ever had a good answer.

One weekend, just to find out what might be possible, with the help of my children, Claire and Emily, we loaded a couple of boxes with jars and took them to an antique store in Iowa City. A pleasant young woman quickly informed us, in effect, that antique fruit jars were as plentiful as flies in a hog lot. Still, if we wanted to leave them, she would try to sell them at two dollars each and split the proceeds with us fifty-fifty. But, she told us sadly, she would have to charge us two dollars apiece to wash the jars, unless we wanted to wash them ourselves. We didn't want to. And we didn't want to pay two dollars each to have them washed in hopes of earning one dollar in return.

So we repacked the jars and took them back to the basement, where hundreds of others like them still stood on the shelves, the counters, the floor, everywhere. They had already been there for decades. Why not leave them awhile longer? The market might still come back. Someday. My father had lived so long and had been right about so many things — the source of the crisis in the farm economy, the reasons for the decline of rail passenger service, the demise of the small town. Why should we doubt his understanding of fruit jars?

After all, anything can happen. Anything. I know a man in Ohio who makes a good living selling tulip bulbs.

THE HOUSE

The little house on the farm my parents bought in 1945 had much in common with the land itself. Both needed immediate restoration. The best thing about the house was the place where it stood — at the north end of a lane that led to a gravel road on the south. Because the house stood so far from the road, the gravel dust that passing cars and trucks raised never soiled the laundry on my mother's clothesline or collected on her windowpanes. From the house and yard, one found a pleasant view in all directions. To the south, the courthouse in Bloomfield lifted its elegant clock tower above the trees. On all sides, one could see the woods, fields, and pastures.

Everyone who saw it agreed that the one-story house occupied a fine location. Unfortunately, that presented its only advantage. In every other respect, the place was a disaster. It lacked electricity, running water, and central heating. The roof leaked. The weatherboard had not felt the caress of a paint brush for many years; it was cracked and worn and in some places barely clung to the house. The doors and windows sagged, admitting blasts of cold air on winter days. A lean-to porch on the north side of the house threatened to collapse at any time. If you dared, you could walk through this porch and go down the steps to the cellar beneath the northwest corner of the house. No one chose to do this, however, because the cellar was full of water in the summer and ice in the winter.

The interior of the house also presented many faults. The floors were scarred and worn. The ugly wallpaper had turned yellow with age. In some places, the plaster had fallen from the ceiling, and more seemed ready to come crashing down at any moment. The woodwork had received too many layers of varnish and now resembled the hull of a poorly tended ship.

Someone with enough money could have easily corrected these deficiencies. My parents didn't have enough money.

My mother suggested borrowing to make the needed repairs, but my father didn't like to borrow. Besides that, he was a perfectionist and wanted to do everything himself. "If I do it, I know it will get done right," he always told her. But because he had a farm to run, plus a full-time job with the railroad, he couldn't find time to make all the repairs on the house himself. Sometimes he had to have help.

The Rural Electrification Administration, one of President Franklin Roosevelt's New Deal programs, had finally reached Davis County, so my parents joined the local cooperative and hired an electrician to wire the house. Next they hired two of my older cousins, Ronald and Gerald Johnson, to tear the porch off the back of the house. These same industrious cousins then dug a trench down the slope to a ditch on the west, laid tile, attached the tile to a drain in the cellar, and filled in the trench. For the first time in decades, the cellar became usable again, although I still preferred not to go down there because of the numerous monsters known to inhabit that fetid cave.

Pete replastered the worst parts of the walls and ceilings. He, my mother, and my sister then painted them. My father hung new doors and installed storm windows. Mother spread rugs on the floors. Pete built a new yard fence on the west side of the house and tore down the old one, thereby moving the barnyard and its noisy inhabitants farther from the house. And there things remained for many years. They had no more money, and my father refused to borrow.

"It would take so little to make the rest of the repairs," my mother sometimes said.

"But if I lost my job and couldn't make the payments, we'd lose everything," Pete said. "Let's wait until we've saved enough." The fear of penury haunted him every day of his adulthood. He had seen it in his father, in his neighbors, and in his own life, and he didn't like the feel of it. "Welcome to the county poor farm," he would joke when people came to visit. But the joke wasn't entirely funny. Its source lay in his own past, and he could not forget that past.

The house had three small rooms on the north side and two larger rooms on the south. We used the three small rooms as a bedroom on the west end, a parlor in the center, and another bedroom on the east. We used the two larger rooms for a front room and a kitchen. A big coal stove provided heat for the two large rooms. A fuel-oil stove in the parlor supplied heat for the three rooms on the north. As I grew older and stronger, it became my task every winter day to bring in the coal and fuel oil for those stoves and keep the fires going. I also brought in water from the well in a metal bucket. A metal dipper rested in the bucket, and all of us drank from that dipper. My mother provided glasses for visitors. The hard water from that metal dipper was the best I have ever tasted.

Thanks to the New Deal, we had electric lights and a radio. On winter evenings, we sat in the parlor and listened to Jack Benny, Groucho Marx, the NBC Symphony Orchestra, or anything else that captured our interest. The shows on radio were so superior to what appears on television today that hardly any intelligent adult who remembers those shows would argue otherwise. In the summer, I sometimes placed the radio in a window in the front room, lay outdoors on the grass, and listened to Harry Caray announce the games for the St. Louis Cardinals.

Finally, my parents saved enough money to begin another phase in the restoration of the house. Men appeared and jacked it up. A bulldozer arrived, burrowed into the backyard, clawed its way under the house, and carved out the space for a basement. Next, the men with the jacks poured a concrete floor and began building the basement walls with one row of concrete blocks for each wall. Then, suddenly, the work stopped. My father didn't like the quality of the men's work and the leisurely pace at which they did it. The men disappeared, and over a period of several months, my father finished building the basement walls himself. By this time, I was old enough to help him by mixing and carrying the mortar, carrying the concrete blocks, and finding the tools he habitually lost. I also became more familiar with his perfectionism. "A little too much sand in that last batch," he said of my mortar.

"Okay," I said, making a mental note to reduce the sand or increase the cement.

"That batch was a little too runny," he said about my next effort.

"All right," I said, making sure to put less water in the next mixture.

"Just a little too thick that time," he said.

I soon learned that if I lived forever I could never mix the mortar my father wanted. He wanted ideal Platonic mortar, but I could produce only average, everyday Davis County mortar.

Eventually, my father finished the basement and built the stairs. My mother immediately wanted running water and a gas furnace, but those would have to wait. Once again, the money had run out. In the meantime, we began work on the living quarters, which could be repaired relatively cheaply if we did the work ourselves. We put up plasterboard, laid floor tiles, and stapled ceiling tiles to long strips of wood. My father gave me the odious task of removing the old varnish from the woodwork with an electric sander. I didn't complain. I knew I wasn't supposed to like it. I was just supposed to do it. Pete then applied a new coat of varnish or, in some rooms, a coat of paint.

With the interior completed, we went outdoors, ripped off all the old weatherboard, and replaced it. Then I painted the entire house white. Two coats. While removing the weatherboard on the south side, we found on the boards beneath it the carefully lettered name of the builder and the date of construction. A man named Lough had erected the house in 1917. He had built a solid house, but anyone could see that the owners had not bothered to keep it in good repair. I can't recall the builder's first name and lack the energy to rip off the new weatherboard to refresh my memory, but he may have been related to the Lough family that owned a farm adjoining ours. You could not have found better neighbors if you had searched the entire continent of North America.

After saving for many more years, Mother got her gas furnace and running water. By that time, I had grown up and left home for college. Finally, my father rebuilt the entire roof — rafters, one-inch boards, tar paper, and shingles. The job was done. The house seemed perfect. But just in time to spoil the celebration, problems emerged in the basement.

It seemed that the single row of concrete blocks erected for the basement walls didn't provide sufficient support, especially in a wet climate such as ours, where the moisture in the soil increased the pressure against the walls, which, in some places, began to buckle inward. The solution, my father learned, was to dig a trench around the entire house, install drainage tile, attach this tile to the drain that ran down the slope to the ditch, push the walls back into place, and fill in the trench. A machine could dig part of this trench, but not all of it. I spent the better part of one summer digging the part the machine couldn't reach. I was still young and the work did me no permanent harm.

Finally, my father began building concrete buttresses in the basement to reinforce the walls. He built the frames, hired a cement truck, and pushed the cement into place with a shovel as it came down the chute through a basement window. He didn't build all these supports at once, but over the years as the need arose.

One mild November day, he was standing on a short stepladder, finishing one of the last of these supports along the north basement wall. The man with the cement truck could watch Pete's progress clearly through the basement window and could therefore release the cement at a pace that was neither too fast nor too slow. My mother stood behind my father, ready, as always, to offer any help needed.

Everything was progressing smoothly, when my father suddenly stopped working and said, "I feel dizzy." He stood there a moment, the shovel dropped from his hands, and he fell backward from the ladder into my mother's arms, where, at the age of seventy, he died.

───────

My parents used to eat at a little café on Church Street in Ottumwa. It was a typical midwestern café, with a counter and stools on one side and wooden booths on the other. Large plate-glass windows in front gave an unimpeded view of the street. As he always did in such places, my father joked with the waitresses, with the cook who was clearly visible through the opening behind the counter, and with the dark-haired man at the cash register who took your money and returned your change. I don't remember the name of the place. The café isn't there anymore. The building itself has been demolished.

One winter day my mother and my aunt Thelma went there for lunch. The waitress came to their booth, placed the menus on the table, and said to my mother, "Where's that ornery husband of yours today?"

Mother hesitated, then said, "Honey, he died three months ago."

The waitress, who didn't even know my father's name, began to cry, and my mother cried with her. Aunt Thelma sat there, unable to speak.

Finally, commerce intruded, as it always does. The waitress took their orders. They ate their lunch, left a tip, paid the bill, and walked out into Church Street, where, in the glare of the sun and the snow, the traffic rolled slowly by.

THE LAST TRAIN

During the last year of her life, in her mind, my mother returned to the CB&Q in Nebraska in the 1930s, to the time that she had once told my sister was the happiest in her life. Every weekday I would leave the office shortly before noon and walk over to see her. If the weather was bad, I would take a bus.

When I walked into her room, I usually found her standing at the window. By a remarkable coincidence, a railroad track passed by about forty yards away. The track had once been part of the central division of the Rock Island Railroad, but by this time the Rock Island was only a memory, and the track was now part of an efficiently operated little line called the Iowa Interstate Railroad, which runs from Chicago to Omaha.

But to my mother, that track belonged to the CB&Q, and in her mind, we lived in a perpetual winter. "Daddy Pete," she said when she heard me enter the room, "I was worried about you."

"I'm fine, Mother," I said, using the form of address that my father, my sister, and I had all used. I kissed her cheek and sat down.

"How is it out on the line?" she said as she sat down across from me. "There's so much snow."

"Everything seems to be getting through," I said.

"I don't see how they can do it."

"I just talked to the towerman in Lincoln," I said, "and he told me thirty-nine was an hour late getting out of there, but thirty-nine is always late getting out of Lincoln because they have to wait for fifteen and then it takes at least ten minutes to transfer the mail, and with this weather it's bound to take longer." I didn't even know what time of day or night thirty-nine had normally left Lincoln in the thirties, but Mother didn't know what time of day it was right then, so it didn't matter, and I could only hope that my imaginary explanation would relieve her fears.

"But it's so cold," she said. She always wore heavy slacks, heavy socks, a blouse, a sweater, and a jacket or coat, but she was still cold, even in July. "What if the switches freeze?"

"Now you have to remember," I said, "that the switches are a lot stronger than they used to be. They just crush the ice, and if anything goes wrong, it triggers those electric signals and the section men get right out there. They're ready for anything on a day like this." I knew practically nothing about the operation of railroad switches, but neither did my mother. Besides, she thought she was talking to my father, and he knew everything about switches. If he said everything was all right with the switches, then everything was all right.

But this didn't prevent her from finding something else to worry about, and I would again splice together what little I knew with what I could invent on the spot. Finally, the time would come when I had to say, "I have to go back to work now, Mother."

She never complained about this. She understood it perfectly. She knew that the work Pete did was crucial and that he had to be there on time. But this didn't stop the tears. "Be careful handing up the orders," she said. "You could slip on the ice and the draft from the train would pull you right under."

"Don't worry about that," I said. "I've spread sand all over that platform, and the engineers are running real slow through Hastings today, even if they don't have to stop. They don't want anybody to get hurt."

"Of course," she said. "They're good about that. But I love you so much, and I worry about you."

"And I love you, Mother. Don't worry. I'll be back soon. Everything will be all right."

Then I went back to my job, which was not crucial to anyone, which served no important purpose, where nobody would ever get hurt, and where my absence on any particular day would inconvenience no one.

On the last day of February in 1996, as I was getting ready for bed, a nurse called and asked to speak to me. "I wondered if anybody would like to come over and sit with Gerata," she said. I said I would come over.

The children were asleep. I put my clothes back on and called my sister in Montgomery. Then I went down to the car and drove across town. It was a quiet night with a hint of spring in the air. The stars were shining. All over the Middle West, renters would begin moving to new farms at daybreak.

I parked the car and got out. A thin layer of snow covered the lawn, but the sidewalks were entirely clear. The nurse met me at the door and let me in. The clock near the entrance said eleven-thirty.

I walked into my mother's room, where she lay unconscious. I sat down on the chair beside the bed and stared at the ruined body of my eighty-eight-year-old mother. The nurse came in and out every few minutes to make sure Mother's back and head remained elevated to allow her to breathe more easily. An Iowa Interstate freight train rolled slowly past and sounded its whistle for the grade crossing at the bottom of the hill.

When the nurse came in, she would talk to my mother. "They think that hearing is the last sense to go," she said. Then she left the room again. I thought about what the nurse had said, but I didn't talk. I couldn't.

At four o'clock in the morning on March 1, 1996, my mother stopped breathing. I went to find the nurse, who was already walking toward the room. She felt for a pulse. She listened for the sound of a heartbeat. "Poor Gerata," she said.

At four o'clock in the morning on March 1, 1996, Amtrak train No. 5, the *California Zephyr*, westbound from Chicago to Oakland, was two hours and twenty-five minutes beyond Salt Lake City, Utah, with stops scheduled all along its 2,425-mile route.

At four o'clock in the morning on March 1, 1996, Amtrak train No. 6, the *California Zephyr*, eastbound from Oakland to Chicago, was thirteen minutes beyond Hastings, Nebraska, via the main line of the old CB&Q, with its next stop scheduled for Lincoln at 5:20 A.M., Central Standard Time.

GOING HOME

In the spring of 2001 my sister and I drove out to Nebraska to find the towns and, if possible, the CB&Q depots where she and my parents had lived in the late 1930s and early 1940s. We could have taken a train, but, of course, the trains don't stop in those towns anymore. Jane had to drive several hundred miles to get to Iowa, but she has limitless energy, and once she decides to do something, a mere five or six hundred miles won't cause her a moment's hesitation. She called from her car while crossing the Mississippi River bridge on Interstate 80. "How much farther is it to your place?" she said.

"Sixty miles," I said. "Don't drive over sixty-five miles an hour. The state police in Iowa are very strict." I had no idea how strict the state police were. Jane was four hours earlier than I had expected, and I needed time to make the apartment look less like a hen house. I slapped clean sheets on the visitor's bed, threw objects into closets, and vacuumed the rug. I briefly considered washing a window or two, but because I hadn't washed any since moving in five years before, I saw no need to get hysterical. Excessive cleanliness dulls the imagination.

We went out to dinner that night with Claire and Emily, and I impressed my sister with my wide circle of friends when a few people I knew paused to say hello. I didn't mention that I never went to any other restaurant, which would have drawn into question the notion that I had a wide circle of friends.

We went to bed at a reasonable hour, and Jane awoke early next morning. I also awoke early because Jane pounded ceaselessly on my door until I stumbled to my feet and made lifelike noises. We went out to breakfast, then headed west in the grand tradition of Lewis and Clark. I had in mind what I thought was a good route. "Let's go to each town in the order in which you lived there," I said. "We can re-create the actual path you followed."

But my sister does not possess the same devotion to historical verisimilitude that I do. "I think we should go all the way to Hastings, then stop at each town as we come to it on the way back," she said. We had already agreed that Hastings was our westernmost destination, given that Pete had worked there so often and given that Hastings was the town from which Mother had foolishly driven off toward Pauline one night in a raging blizzard while little Jane slept in the backseat. After brief negotiations, we agreed to follow the route Jane preferred. We came to this agreement largely because we were riding in her car and she was driving.

We drove 250 miles across Iowa's fertile, gently rolling landscape through weather that only midwesterners love. Tumultuous rain clouds bearing explosions of lightning came out of the west and drenched the black earth that is the source of our wealth and our happiness. Then the clouds passed and the blue half-sphere of the sky engulfed us. Not everyone would like our state, and frankly that doesn't trouble us overmuch. We're accustomed to being misunderstood. We confess that you will see no mountain peaks in Iowa, no ocean waves breaking on sandy beaches, no redwood forests, no waterfalls hundreds of feet high. But in addition, you will see no hurricanes, no tidal waves, no volcanic eruptions, no mud slides, no avalanches, and no earthquakes stronger than a ripple. And please, if you can, show me a beach that will produce two hundred bushels of corn per acre.

So on we drove, across the Missouri River into Nebraska. Southwest of Omaha, we paused to gaze at the Platte, a river so wide that one finds it hard to believe that it is no deeper than your kitchen sink. Yet I have often peered at a photograph of my sister and my cousin Carroll, standing in the middle of that river when they were only three or four years old. Although they both looked angelic, I know they could not walk on water, so I have to believe that the Platte River is truly as shallow as everyone claims.

Although Jane and I had bypassed Omaha, we stopped in Lincoln, for this is where our family's romance with the railroad had begun on that day in 1937 when Pete Irelan stepped off the train at Lincoln Station. We drove around happily. The town belonged to us. I took photographs of the most beautiful statue of Abraham Lincoln I have ever seen — cast in black, head bowed, hands clasped in front. The statue stands on the Capitol grounds in front of a large granite block on which are inscribed the words of the Gettysburg Address.

But we didn't happen to see Lincoln Station, not that we were in a hurry. Finally, as night came on, we drove to a motel near I-80, where a young clerk eagerly rented us two rooms and gave us precise directions, along with a map, to Lincoln Station. But the next morning, adhering faithfully to our plan, we set off for Hastings. Lincoln Station would remain standing until we returned.

We drove eighty miles on down I-80, past fields of young corn and soybeans, turned south on Route 281, and drove the remaining twenty miles to Hastings, population twenty-two thousand. We had arrived by this point at what was unmistakably the Great Plains. Jack and Jill would search in vain for a hill down which to fall in central Nebraska.

When we reached Hastings, we followed the signs directing us to the Amtrak depot, fearing all the while what might have happened to it since the glory days of CB&Q passenger service. Perhaps the original building no longer existed. But when we reached the station, we found something more wonderful than I had ever expected. Some preservation-minded group or governmental agency had gone to a great deal of trouble and expense to restore the depot. The lovely Spanish Colonial building displayed a low-pitched red-tile roof, sand-colored walls of stone and stucco, decorative flourishes around the doors and windows, and a low porch that encircled the whole depot.

I eagerly took out my camera and used an entire thirty-six-exposure roll of film to photograph the depot from every conceivable angle. As I stood on the side of the building that faces the track, I heard a train approaching from behind me. My sister shouted something to me about the train, but I couldn't hear what. She shouted again, and I turned just in time to see and photograph a green caboose bearing the logo of the Burlington Northern Railroad. But I saw no mention of the Santa Fe. The caboose was one merger out of date. Freight trains don't usually pull cabooses anymore, but this one did. Jane and I had seen two miracles in one day: a beautiful functioning depot and a train pulling a caboose. Perhaps a volcano would suddenly rise from the cornfields.

Unfortunately, the agent had locked the depot. The *California Zephyr* stops at Hastings in the middle of the night, whether eastbound or westbound. Sometimes both trains meet there. Amtrak arranges the timetable this way so tourists can pass through the Rocky Mountains during daylight hours. I would rather see the Hastings depot than the Donner Pass, but Amtrak knows what it's doing, and any trainload of passengers would shout down my preference. In any event, the depot had no need for an agent at the hour when Jane and I arrived, and I

Pete Irelan frequently worked as an agent in this Chicago, Burlington &
Quincy depot in Hastings, Nebraska, during the late 1930s and early 1940s.
After two mergers, the Burlington Railroad is now the Burlington Northern
Santa Fe. Amtrak still uses this lovely building as a passenger depot.
Photograph by Patrick Irelan, 2001.

didn't think the authorities would want me to break down the door merely to photograph the interior.

I was putting another roll of film into the camera when Jane said, "Pat, we still have to see Pauline and Murphy today."

"Wouldn't you like to be photographed standing in front of the agent's bay?" I said.

"No." My sister can be quite stubborn. Our dear mother also possessed this trait.

I finished loading the camera and got into the car. As we drove out of Hastings, I pointed out many buildings I wanted to photograph, but the woman behind the wheel refused to apply her foot to the brakes, and those buildings will remain forever lost in obscurity.

Pauline stands about fifteen miles south of Hastings, and we arrived there quickly. Here we met with complete failure. We couldn't find the depot. We couldn't even find a railroad track, although we did cross the old roadbed. Jane stopped the car, and I got out to look up and down the length of the former railroad in hopes of seeing something to photograph as a reminder of the distant 1930s. But there was nothing. None of this surprised us. Pauline had stood on a spur line, and railroads lost interest in spur lines shortly after they built them. We drove around the tiny village and saw no one on the streets. We saw no store or business of any kind — only a few houses, and many of those looked abandoned. Where, I wondered, was the cheerful section man who had come out in that blizzard so many years before to make sure that Mrs. Irelan and little Jane arrived safely? Where was he buried? What stone had been erected in his honor?

Finally, Jane said, "Why don't you just take a picture of the sign at the edge of town?" I took the picture. The sign says

PAULINE

UNINC.

Our visit to Pauline left us subdued. We drove back north and turned east toward Murphy. When we arrived, I saw that Murphy looked even smaller than my mother's descriptions of it during my childhood, but you couldn't miss it unless you were asleep. The same grain elevator still rises triumphantly from the flatness of the plains. And at the top of the elevator, with the letters arranged vertically, someone has painted the word MURPHY in large black capital letters. The town has shrunk, yet the elevator has grown to twice its size since my parents and sister moved there in 1937, and it is the old section that still bears the word MURPHY.

But as we expected, everything else had changed. The depot Mother operated had vanished. The grocery store where my father had gone to buy bread and coffee for the thirteen migrant workers had gone with the depot. We hoped to find someone who could tell us if the depot had been moved, but the only business in town was the grain elevator, and the office had closed for the day. We stood there like the orphans we were, staring up at the elevator, the only reminder of the adventure that had started on that spot for my mother and sister. I took fifteen pictures of the grain elevator. A coal train from Wyoming roared past. I didn't count the cars. There would be about 130. There always were.

<hr>

The next day we drove back east to Milford, a town of about two thousand people. We quickly found the main line of the Burlington Northern Santa Fe, but as expected, the depot had disappeared. Despite its relatively small size, Milford appeared to be flourishing. The houses looked in good repair. The main street offered stores, a gas station, a post office, a bank, and, most important, a senior center on a corner lot. What better place to find someone who would remember what had become of the depot? Jane parked the car, and I walked to the door at the corner of the brick building. Locked. Locked doors seemed ready to block our every attempt to rediscover the heroic Irelan past.

I looked down the sidewalk. Near the back of the senior center, seven or eight people stood beside an open door. Some were children, some were teenagers, and some were middle-aged adults. None of them paid any attention to me. This reminded me that many people in our broad nation contend that Midwesterners are cold and unfriendly. I prepared myself to test this often-stated and slanderous notion.

I walked down the sidewalk and stopped a few feet from the person who looked the oldest — a woman about forty or forty-five whose dark-brown hair showed a touch of gray. "Excuse me," I said. "My sister and I are trying to find the Burlington depot that our mother operated back in the thirties." I motioned down the street toward my sister. After a slight pause, all the adults began talking to me and each other about the possible location of the depot. This matter had suddenly become the most important issue in their lives. They tried to remember who had bought the depot and where that person had taken it. But, everyone agreed, we should go downstairs and ask the rest of the family. Everyone was there. Someone would know. I should go get my sister and join them at the birthday party for their eighty-year-old mother. I objected that we couldn't intrude on their party. They denied that it was an intrusion.

I went to fetch my sister, and the children and adults led us down the stairs to the party room in the basement of the senior center. They introduced us to their beautiful white-haired mother and grandmother, and we shook hands and said happy birthday. They had us sign the guest book. They had us write our names on paper stars, which they then taped to the wall with all the others. They gave us cake and coffee. Everyone soon learned why we had come to Milford, and they all tried desperately to remember where the depot now sat.

My sister went off to talk to everyone she could. A man about thirty or thirty-five walked over and said hello to me. He wore a long, reddish-brown beard and a friendly smile. Like everyone else in the room, he knew by then that my parents had worked for the CB&Q. After we exchanged pleasantries, he said, "I'm a third-generation worker in the Burlington repair shops in Lincoln." I noticed that he said "Burlington" and not "Burlington Northern Santa Fe." It's difficult to remember a new name for something, and a new name also brings bad luck, as my father wisely taught me. It's safer to forget the new name.

I asked the man with the long beard about his work. Despite his youth, he had already risen to a supervisory position. Although he didn't say it, I knew this meant that he could teach the younger workers how to repair almost every part of every car on the Burlington Railroad. I expressed my sincere admiration for the man's success. I wanted to talk to him longer, but just then the first woman I had spoken to walked up. A consensus had arisen. Everyone now remembered who had bought the depot and that he had moved it into the country south of town and turned it into a house. Then the woman gave me precise instructions about how to find it. I thanked her and shook hands. I said good luck and shook hands with the man with the long beard. I said happy birthday again to the family matriarch.

My sister, who has more charm than all the representatives to the United Nations, had already become the best friend of most of the people in the room. She said thank-you to everyone and apologized for disrupting the party. Everyone denied that we had disrupted anything. We waved good-bye to everybody and climbed the stairs to the sidewalk. As we walked to the car, Jane asked, "Did you get the name of that family?"

"No," I said. "Did you?"

"No."

It was too late to go back and ask, so we drove west out of Milford, past the new high school at the edge of town, past the city limits, and turned left onto a gravel road. We drove about three and a half miles until we saw an abandoned building on the right side of the road. Jane pulled into the driveway, and I got out to look around. The building looked vaguely like a small depot. It also looked vaguely like a small house. Finally, it looked vaguely like a depot that someone had turned into a house. A portion of the wall near the front door had been converted into a wide set of windows. Someone could have replaced the agent's bay window with these windows. I thought we had followed the directions correctly. This had to be the old depot. I took the lens cap off the camera and recorded the find for future generations. Then I climbed back into the car. But one lingering doubt remained. The family in Milford had said nothing about the house being abandoned. Who would buy an old depot, spend the money to convert it into a house, and then abandon it? Maybe we hadn't followed the directions correctly. We needed more information, and both Jane and I saw where to find it.

Directly across the road stood a large farmhouse that gave every indication of being inhabited. We drove across the road and parked beside a large oak tree. Or maybe it was an elm or maple. My mind was occupied with depots. I walked to the door and knocked. No one came. I knocked again. Still no one. I turned and looked at the hayfield beyond the house and barn. A young farmer no older than thirty was baling hay with what looked like an old Farmall baler, a baler so old that it produced small rectangular bales like the ones I remembered from my boyhood. I had seen the young man from across the road, but had hoped to find the answer to my question without having to interrupt his work. Now I would again have to challenge the foul notion that midwesterners are cold and unfriendly.

The young man saw me coming, but he kept working until I had almost reached the tractor and baler. Then he stopped, shut off the baler, turned off the tractor, and climbed down. "Sorry to bother you," I said, "but my sister and I drove over from Iowa to find the old Milford depot where our mother worked back in the thirties. Is that it across the road?" We do not begin conversations with small talk in the Middle West after interrupting someone at work. We come straight to the point.

"No," the man said. "That's not it." He paused a moment to reflect. "You need to go back north to the first intersection and turn right," he said, gesturing northward with the cap in his right hand as he wiped the sweat from his forehead with his left hand. "Then go about half a mile and look for a building on the left side of the road. You can't miss it. There's a pond beside it and the word 'Milford' is still painted on the east gable end."

"Okay," I said. "That's where we went wrong. We went through one too many intersections, and we didn't turn east." The time for small talk had arrived, brief small talk. "I haven't seen bales like that for years," I said, pointing at one of the small bales secured by two strands of binder twine. "I used to stack them in haymows."

"I sell them to people with horses," he said. "There's no point in buying one of those thousand-pound bales when all you own is one or two horses. You can't even get a big bale inside a barn or stable to keep it out of the weather. I can get $3.50 apiece for these small bales."

Time to end small talk. "Well, thanks," I said. "Sorry to interrupt."

"That's all right," he said. "Watch that electric fence around the garden."

"I will. Thanks. So long."

"So long." He started back toward the tractor and baler. I watched him enviously for a moment as he walked away. He had fair skin but the good sense to wear a cap and a long-sleeve shirt. He was smart, healthy, and a hard worker. He would do well. The tractor started, then the rhythmic whir of the baler. I turned away.

As advised, I avoided the electric fence, just as I had on the way out to the field. Electric fences shock but do not kill animals or humans. They protect gardens or other enclosures from sheep, cattle, horses, and deer, but not rabbits. Rabbits go under them. I have no data on elephants or buffalo.

Five minutes later, we pulled into the driveway of the Milford depot, now converted into a house, with the name "Milford" clearly visible on the east gable end. We had scored our first and only success after two failures at Pauline and Murphy. I knocked on the door to ask permission to take photos. No one came. I turned on the camera and took

*Gerata Hunter Irelan operated this Burlington Railroad depot in Milford,
Nebraska, from October of 1939 to March of 1941. The depot has since
been moved south of town and converted into a house, but the owner has
proudly retained the name "Milford" on the east gable end.
Photograph by Patrick Irelan, 2001.*

enough pictures to keep Kodak in business for six weeks. Then we
drove back to Lincoln, tired, hungry, and as smug as bandits.

━━━━━━━━

The next morning, we had one final task to perform: a thorough inspection of Lincoln Station, the building where our father had learned
how to send all boxcars to the right locations, hand up train orders to
speed-loving engineers, and keep a depot clean and tidy. We slept well
and arrived at Lincoln Station late in the morning, just as a farmers'
market was breaking up. "How'd you do?" I said to a red-haired man
who was putting his gear into a pickup.

He leaned against the truck and said, "I sold everything I could and
gave the rest away. It'll all be rotten by next weekend anyway. I'm not

much of a businessman." Then he laughed at his own self-criticism, thereby revealing the actual truth. He'd made good money that morning, but wouldn't admit it to anyone but his wife. All the other vendors had counted up their proceeds, and a festive atmosphere filled the parking lot in front of Lincoln Station. Comments about this or that dealer's lousy tomatoes sent waves of laughter through the crowd.

I turned my attention to Lincoln Station. Jane and I walked all the way around the long, three-story building. We went inside and talked to the ladies in the visitors' center. Then Jane wandered off to raid some nearby shops while I studied the refurbished oak woodwork in the station. I looked through the windows of the locked doors at the expansive waiting room, which stood ready for a banquet with linen-covered tables, folded napkins sticking out of crystal glasses like white crocuses, and perfectly placed plates, cups, and silverware. The people of Lincoln had done a good job of preserving Lincoln Station, but it really wasn't a train station anymore. To buy a train ticket, you had to walk back outside and go down the platform to the north end of the building, where Amtrak had erected a small addition. The builders had done a good job of blending the addition into the old station, using matching bricks and windows. But the thought of building a train station that was nothing more than an addition to an already existing station caused me an unpleasant moment of confusion.

On the other hand, many people had actually done something to save and restore a beautiful building. They had gone to endless meetings, written letters, raised money. What had I done? Nothing. So I put these critical thoughts aside and replaced them with gratitude to those people who actually do something instead of just talking about it. I felt better. People had gotten off their couches and done something. I began to feel like Lincoln, Nebraska's, foremost booster. Sentiments like these inevitably cause me to reach for the camera and start looking for photo angles.

On the side of the station facing the tracks, I found a line of antique cars and an ancient engine that appeared to form a permanent display. This brought me little pleasure. I share the conductor's dismay for a train that isn't in motion, and this train gave every indication of being attached to that spot for the rest of eternity. So I walked around to the front of the building, where I found that the light was perfect when one viewed the station from the southeast. From that angle, I could capture the entire length of the building beneath a blue sky and soft white clouds.

As I photographed this scene, with the vendors from the farmers' market still cleaning up, an unexpected feeling came over me. My sister and I had come home. I looked around for a black-haired man in a crisp blue suit and a silk tie. He, too, would be full of hope like these joking vendors. He would go anywhere, to any depot, and work any hours to support his family, because that was what a man was supposed to do in 1937. He would learn everything there was to know about passenger trains, freight trains, tariffs, signals, train orders, freight orders, timetables, complaining customers, and grateful customers. In only four months, he would become a railroad man for life, and nothing on earth would ever be better, more useful, more important, and more deserving of the best he could do.

I looked again, but, of course, he wasn't there. I walked over to one of the glass and steel awnings suspended over the two front doors by steel rods anchored to the wall. There should be a brass plaque here, I thought. It should read

IN THIS BUILDING IN 1937,
PETE IRELAN BECAME A RAILROAD MAN,
AND IN HIS MEMORY WE MARK THIS SPOT
TO HONOR HIM AND ALL THOSE LIKE HIM
WHO HANDED UP THE ORDERS
AND KEPT THE DISPATCHERS HAPPY.

But I saw no such plaque and never would. I found my sister, got into the car, and put the camera away. We drove out of Lincoln and headed south and east toward Nebraska City and the bridge across the Missouri River to Iowa. We would drive across the state to Davis and Wapello counties. Uncle Kenny would be waiting to see us on the farm, and Aunt Mabel would be waiting at her house in Ottumwa. The air smelled of black earth and newly cut timothy. Spring is so lovely in the Middle West. The crops, pastures, and leaves take on a rich, intense greenness. Our trip would soon be over. And everywhere we stopped, we would meet friendly people, who would answer every question and show us every kindness.

Index

Adcock, Curtis, 125
Albia, Iowa, 88
Allerton, Iowa, 112, 113, 116
Ash Grove, Iowa, 7, 82, 83, 106; Ash
   Grove School, 8

Baker, Meta Irelan; photograph of,
   103
Bear Creek, 8
Bircher, Emmett, 73–74, 80–82
Birmingham, Iowa, 46
Bloomfield, Iowa, 8, 11, 24, 49, 51,
   138; *Bloomfield Democrat*, 102, 103;
   Bloomfield High School, 11, 65, 76,
   77, 105, 133
Brown, H. C., 67
Burlington Northern Santa Fe Rail-
   road. *See* Burlington Railroad *and*
   CB&Q Railroad.
Burlington Railroad, 9, 27. *See also*
   CB&Q Railroad.
Burlington Zephyrs, 37
Buttontown Grade School, 75, 77

California Zephyr, 44, 125, 145, 148
CB&Q (Chicago, Burlington, and
   Quincy) Railroad, 27, 31, 39–40,
   43, 48, 112, 125, 127, 143, 146–57
Cassill, R. V., 106–107
Chillicothe, Missouri, 11, 19, 24
Clay College, 105

Davis County, Iowa, 8, 11, 17, 20, 21,
   87, 93
Davis County Republican, 16, 17
Des Moines, Iowa, 89; *Des Moines
   Register*, 51, 88

Des Moines River, 2, 87, 89, 108, 112,
   125
Drakesville, Iowa, 1, 2, 102; Drakesville Elementary School, 2

Eldon, Iowa, 112

Fairfield, Iowa, 46
Fenton, Charles, 63–67
Fimmen, W. R., 20, 25
Fleming, Barton; photograph of, 84
Fleming, Clarence; photograph of,
   84
Fleming, Gilford; photograph of, 84
Fleming, John, 83; photograph of, 84
Fleming, Susan Adcock, 83; photo-
   graph of, 84
Fleming, Wray; photograph of, 84
Fox River, 51

Golden State Limited, 116–17, 128

Hadley, Jill Ann, 137
Hadley, Lisa Jane, 137
Hadley, Sara Jane, 137
Harris, Donald, 20, 25, 26
Harshfield, Blanche, 75
Hastings, Nebraska, 36, 38, 146–47,
   148
Haynes, John, 47
History of Davis County, 101–102, 104
Hopewell Cemetery, 6, 86
Houk, Helen Wells, 66
Hunter, Austa Fleming, 6–7, 77, 82–
   86, 98; photograph of, 84, 97
Hunter, Carroll, 147
Hunter, Chester, 10

Hunter, Gene, 77
Hunter, Joan, 77
Hunter, Justin, 22
Hunter, Kenneth (Kenny), 3–5, 6, 16,
    22, 35, 77; photograph of, 97
Hunter, Laris, 6–7, 83, 88, 96–98;
    photograph of, 97
Hunter, Larry, 9–10
Hunter, Lily Herteen, 3, 16, 35, 77
Hunter, Melvin Elwood, 7
Hunter, Thelma, 3–5, 8, 9–10, 95–
    100, 142; photograph of, 97

Iowa City, Iowa, 135, 137
Irelan, Blanche Kough, 72, 78–79
Irelan, C. G. (Pete), 4–5, 11–15, 16–
    23, 31–34, 72, 112–13, 134–36,
    139–42; photograph of, 13, 18, 41
Irelan, Charles, 102; photograph of,
    103
Irelan, Claire Elizabeth, 10, 103, 125–
    29, 137, 146
Irelan, Claude, 109
Irelan, Clayton, 75
Irelan, Clell, 105–11, 135; photograph
    of, 110
Irelan, Cliff, 66, 72–73, 78–79
Irelan, Elizabeth Jane, 101–103;
    photograph of, 103
Irelan, Emily Jane, 103, 137, 146
Irelan, George; photograph of, 103
Irelan, Gerata Hunter, 6–10, 16–23,
    37–39, 80–81, 136–37, 143–45;
    photograph of, 18, 97
Irelan, Henry; photograph of, 103
Irelan, Jane, 21, 35, 53, 130–33, 146–
    57; photograph of, 41
Irelan, Mabel Cassill, 105–107, 111,
    135, 136–37
Irelan, Marion, 1, 47, 74–75, 102, 104;
    photograph of, 103
Irelan, Max, 79
Irelan, Pete. *See* C. G. Irelan.
Irelan, Susan Hudgens, 1–2, 47,
    74–75

Irelan, Thomas, 75; photograph of,
    103
Irelan, William, 101–104; photograph
    of, 103
IXL Grade School, 105

John Morrell and Company, 106, 108,
    109
Johnson, Dottla Hunter, 4, 96, 106–
    107; photograph of, 97
Johnson, Gerald, 139
Johnson, Ronald, 139

Keosauqua, Iowa, 22, 124–25

La Salle Street Station, 117, 128, 129
Lewis, John L., 88
Lincoln, Abraham, 60–61, 147
Lincoln, Nebraska, 27, 147, 155
Lincoln Station, 147–48, 155–57
Lock, Norma Irelan, 72
Lough family, 141

McElderry, Merve, 47
McMillin, Eva, 67
McReynolds, Alice Irelan; photo-
    graph of, 103
Milford, Nebraska, 35, 151–55
Milligan, Donald C., 65
Minoletti, Jacquelyn Johnson, 7
Mississippi River, 87
Moore, Bert, 49
Moore, H. H., 63
Mount Pleasant, Iowa, 46
Murphy, Nebraska, 28–29, 31, 43,
    150–51
Mystic, Iowa, 126

Newton, Iowa, 72, 78

Oman, Jennifer Lock, 72
Ottumwa, Iowa, 1, 2, 21, 35, 36, 85,
    98, 110, 125, 132, 142; Irving Ele-
    mentary School, 98; Ottumwa
    Hospital, 9, 21, 48